I have always admired the ministry of Dr. Charles Roesel. I had heard so much about his church meeting the needs of people that many churches would shy away from I could not believe it until I met Dr. Roesel himself. His passion to reach the down and out, the misfits, the outcast, and the misunderstood is directly from the heart of God. As a matter of fact, Dr. Roesel's ministry has proven to be the hands, the legs, the feet, and the heart of Jesus Christ! What Dr. Roesel and his ministry have done in Florida is truly "A God Thing"!

Fred Luter

Pastor, Franklin Avenue Baptist Church, New Orleans, LA.
President, Southern Baptist Convention

Can a church meet the needs of those most at risk in its community and do so without watering down the gospel? The answer is absolutely yes, and no one has demonstrated that better than Charles Roesel and his congregation at First Baptist Leesburg. Roesel has led the way with multiple ministries that are giving people the immediate help they need to change their circumstances while also introducing them to the life-transforming Savior who will change their lives. Roesel's enthusiasm and love for people electrifies his ministry, and it spills over onto the pages of this book. What would our nation and world look like if more churches followed the biblical mandate to serve the "least of these"? I hope thousands of pastors take this book to heart so we might find out.

Kevin Ezell

President, North American Mission Board

Charles Roesel has been modeling ministries of mercy for decades. This book tells the amazing story, but also provides you direction about how you and your church can be involved in serving the poor and hurting. When it comes to showing and sharing the love of Jesus, Charles is worth listening to.

Ed Stetzer

Author of *Subversive Kingdom* www.edstetzer.com

I have always been a fan of Dr. Charles Roesel. I have used him to speak at my churches and found him to be a man of vision, compassion, and passion.

His ministry has been one that has been like that of Jesus Christ. He believes that a church and believers ought to minister to the whole person. His example is truly one to be admired and followed.

Frank Page

Executive Committee, Southern Baptist Convention

If you want to see the future, read this amazing story of Pastor Charles Roesel. He built his ministry on ministry evangelism before ministry evangelism was cool. He was not in an urban center or a great city where you would most expect to find a ministry like his. He showed us how a church in any setting will reach people for Christ when they make meeting the needs of people outside the church the priority inside the church. The journey toward becoming a fruitful church requires time to learn the ministry model pioneered by Dr. Charles Roesel. Do not miss the story of a man who should be a hero for all who love evangelism.

Chuck Kelley, Th.D.
President, New Orleans Baptist Theological Seminary

The first time I met Pastor Roesel, I commented on how wonderful the ministry of the Christian Care center was. He looked at me and said, "It's a God thing." He had been an excellent Pastor Emeritus and encourager of the ministry as it continues to move forward. You'll be blessed by reading the life-changing stories in the book, *It's a God Thing*. May the Lord use it to birth the seeds of a ministry evangelism awakening in your church.

Cliff Lea
Senior Pastor, First Baptist Church, Leesburg, Florida

Dr. Charles Roesel reminds us what ministry and evangelism are supposed to look like. At what point did we decide the Christian faith was merely propositional truth detached from the real lives of real people? I'm not sure, but It's a God Thing reminds us of God's heart for people – regardless of their circumstances or choices in life – and how Christians and churches can come into alignment with His heart. My consistent thought as I read this book was: Any church can do this, and every church should do this!

Larry D. Robertson
President, Tennessee Baptist Convention

Charles Roesel is a major rediscoverer of what Peter Drucker would have called Christianity's "main business." In an age when countless churches are stuck in routines, spinning their wheels and majoring on one minor or another, this book will help thousands of churches find their way into a powerful future.

George G. Hunter III
Dean and Distinguished Professor Emeritus,
School of World Mission and Evangelism,
Asbury Theological Seminary

This book is a game changer for churches today! Charles Roesel doesn't just write about ministry evangelism, he lives it. Following this example and through a clear biblical call, churches can engage people with the gospel in a fresh way. If you want to see your city transformed by the power of the gospel, this book is a must read.

Nathan Lorick
Director of Evangelism, Southern Baptists of Texas Convention

This is a fresh new motivational and informational book which will give you great insight into the how-to's of growing a strong *intentionally evangelistic* New Testament church.

From easy reading of how someone has actually done it, to the overwhelming sophisticated work of God's Holy Spirit in your life and ministry, this book will give you what you need to apply the directives of the great commission.

We are often looking for ways and basic biblical principles to pushing back the darkness and making Satan mad… Well, here it is! Read with a pen in hand, mark everything that touches your heart, look for the application in your own ministry, and then DO IT!

David Burton
Evangelism Lead Strategist, Florida Baptist Convention

I have known and worked with Dr. Charles Roesel for almost twenty years. He is the real deal. He has and still does eat and sleep "Ministry Evangelism." He has been and continues to be our best "cheer leader" as well as providing a practical book on the "why and how to" for those interested in seeing people saved through the use of ministry evangelism. Thank you Charles for your years of faithful service and the encouragement you provide for all of us.

Sammy Gilbreath
Alabama Baptist Convention State Board of Missions

This book is an absolute MUST READ. Seminary students, church planters, pastors seeking to grow or revitalize a church, and laypersons serious about reaching and ministering to their communities for Christ will find it invaluable. Thank you, thank you, thank you Dr. Roesel for writing this book!

Douglas K. Dieterly
Chairman of the Board of Trustees,
North American Mission Board, SBC

It's A God Thing

The Powerful Results of Ministry Evangelism

Charles L. Roesel

ANEKO Press

www.lifesentencepublishing.com

Visit Charles's website: www.ministryevangelism.org

It's a God Thing – Charles L. Roesel

Printed in the United States of America

First edition published 2013

LIFE SENTENCE Publishing books are available at discounted prices for ministries and other outreach. Find out more by contacting info@lifesentencepublishing.com

LIFE SENTENCE Publishing and its logo are trademarks of

LIFE SENTENCE Publishing, LLC
P.O. Box 652
Abbotsford, WI 54405

Paperback ISBN: 978-1-62245-148-7

Ebook ISBN: 978-1-62245-149-4

10 9 8 7 6 5 4 3 2 1

This book is available from
www.lifesentencepublishing.com, www.amazon.com,
Barnes & Noble, and your local Christian bookstore.

Cover Image: Alina Cardiae Photography/Shutterstock.com

Cover Design: Amber Burger

Editor: Sheila Wilkinson, Ruth Zetek

Share this book on Facebook:

Contents

I would like to acknowledge and thank the following persons:

First of all, my lovely wife and partner in ministry for over fifty-five years, who is the greatest prayer warrior I know.

Ruth Ann Suber, who patiently took hours of dictation from me and typed the original manuscript of this book.

Kevin Ezell, Al Gilbert, Jerry Daniel, and J. Ryan West, who have done incredible work on this project and have been some of my greatest encouragers. I was amazed at how quickly our leader, Kevin, made the decision to make this project a reality.

The First Baptist Church of Leesburg, Florida, which is a fellowship of burning hearts created by the Holy Spirit, without whom this project would have never happened.

Samuel and Tim, for their extensive research in preparing the foreword of this book. It set the tone for the entire work.

My many friends across the Southern Baptist Convention, who have enthusiastically encouraged me to write this book.

Wonderful men of God who shared truths that have impacted my life. I always remember the truths, but not always the sources. Having been in the ministry sixty-plus years, it has been my privilege to hear some of the greatest preachers in the nation. I owe them a debt of gratitude, and though I cannot remember many of the names of these heroes, I want to say thank-you for the impact you have made on my life.

The Great Story

The story of First Baptist Church, Leesburg, Florida, is a God thing. It is the story of the dynamic, miraculous power of our loving God. This large Southern Baptist Church has a sixteen-bed Children's Shelter Home, a thirty-bed Men's Residence, a sixteen-bed Women's Care Center, a Benevolence Center that serves 2,000 people food and clothing every month, a Pregnancy Care Center that serves 250 people per month, a medical center with ninety doctors volunteering and serving more than 600 per month, and a refurbished motel – the Samaritan Inn – that offers free accommodations for up to eight homeless families at a time.

The ministries are operated through the Christian Care Center, a $1.3-million-per-year charitable organization owned by the church. Several of the church's ministries became a community effort over the last thirty years, supported and staffed by many Christians who volunteer their time. These efforts would not exist, however, if it were not for the leadership of Pastor Emeritus Charles L. Roesel.

At a time when the excesses of Walter Rauschenbusch's "social gospel" scared many away from mercy ministries, Charles Roesel believed Matthew 25:31-46 gave a clear command to care for the poor and needy in his community, and he led his church to be faithful to this biblical message.

Pastor Roesel experienced the act of mercy even before his

birth. His mother's doctor said that her life was at risk and she should abort the pregnancy. She chose to honor God with the pregnancy. Through the miraculous power of God, both lived, and Roesel's mother believed God had something special for him to do.

This choice was but one example of mercy that characterized the Roesel family. They also provided a free place for needy people in their home. Their family always had someone living with them, and through such acts of mercy, Roesel's parents taught him to love without limit.

God continued to shape Roesel, molding him into a compassionate pastor with a heart for poor and neglected people. While training for the ministry at the Southern Baptist Theological Seminary, he did some chaplaincy work at Ormsby Village for Boys. One day, as he taught the Lord's Prayer, he pointed out that God is our heavenly Father. One boy jumped up and said, "If God is like my father, I don't want to have anything to do with him." The boy stormed out of the room, which broke Roesel's heart.

In addition to his role as a chaplain, Roesel served as pastor to a church that reached out to poverty-ridden families in the Appalachian Mountains. This ministry helped Roesel develop his insight into ministering to the poor through a local church. Growing up in a mercy-oriented family carried over to his choices, and God used these experiences to shape him for the heart of his pastorate: Ministry Evangelism.

After seminary, Roesel became pastor of a church in New Smyrna Beach, Florida, where the church took *ministry evangelism* to the beach where beach-goers often got their cars stuck in the sand. Because towing companies could charge whatever they wanted, Roesel and his church saw an opportunity to minister to people's physical needs. They built a dune buggy and offered to pull folks out of the sand for free. After blessing people in this way, they would tell them about the wonderful love of Christ.

At his next pastorate, Pastor Roesel kept the soft spot in his heart for the marginalized and less fortunate. In the early 1970s, First Baptist of Zephyrhills, Florida, established a home for abused girls and reached three hundred and fifty young girls with food, clothing, shelter, and the love of Christ in the few years of his ministry there. God continued to burden him to minister to the "least of these" and blessed his efforts to meet needs and share Christ with neglected people.

Then, Pastor Roesel received a phone call from First Baptist Church in Leesburg, Florida. He says, "I didn't want to go to Leesburg. I was in a church where attendance had increased from two hundred to twelve hundred, and fourteen hundred people had been baptized in the last ten years. We had a fantastic ministry." He continued, "But I told the Lord that if the call was unanimous, I'd consider it His will. I thought I was safe because they hadn't done anything unanimously in a long time."

I had to be faithful even though I could not see why God wanted me to pastor that church.

God had other plans. After a unanimous vote, Roesel found a church that was "wired together by organization, frozen together by formality, and rusted together by tradition." He accepted the invitation from First Baptist to be the church's pastor, but realized quickly that the deadness of the church produced dead results. Attendance had dropped by 50 percent to about two hundred people. It was landlocked and over one hundred years old.

Pastor Roesel said, "Any church-growth book would have discouraged one from going there. I really did not want to go. I was happy where I was. I knew, however, that God had called me there, and I had to be faithful even though I could not see why God wanted me to pastor that church."

At the end of his first sermon, he asked the congregation to join hands and sing "Sweet, Sweet Spirit." That afternoon a man called and told him that he didn't want the church to become charismatic. Another church had reportedly started holding hands and singing just before they went charismatic. He also said it wasn't right for the pastor to ask them to hold hands with another man's wife because "You know what's on a man's mind when he holds another man's wife's hand."

Well, Pastor Roesel said he knew what that man was thinking; he'd just confessed it. The next week Roesel apologized and said he wanted to be more biblical. He then asked the congregation to greet each other with a holy kiss. After all, that is what God's Word teaches. That broke the ice, and thus began what would eventually become a fantastic ministry. But for five years, they resisted *ministry evangelism* because of the existing mentality.

Pastor Roesel wanted to build a children's home. He recalled: "One man offered the building; another offered the money. It barely passed – by 51 percent. That was no way to start." Many opposed the ministry. He was reminded of the old saying, "I don't mind being swallowed by a whale – but I hate to be nibbled to death by minnows." Although the culture clash continued for several years, Roesel pastored faithfully, seeking to lead the congregation toward *ministry evangelism*.

While sharing his vision to care for the poor, Pastor Roesel practiced traditional forms of evangelism, and the church grew steadily. They set a high attendance goal of three hundred for the day he preached his trial sermon and exceeded that goal.

Four months later, they set a new goal. Roesel asked several leaders, "What should be the goal?" One said four hundred. The pastor asked, "Can we reach that?"

The reply: "It'd be a piece of cake."

The pastor then said, "Then that would not be a worthy goal."

Another said, "What about five hundred?"

Once again, the question: "Can we reach that?"

The reply: "We can do that."

"Then that is not a worthy goal," the pastor said.

Another responded, "What about six hundred?"

Again, the question: "Can we reach that?"

The response: "That would take a miracle."

The pastor then said, "Then that is a worthy goal. We want to see a God thing!" The church had 601 that Sunday. It doubled in size – from 301 to 601 in four months – which was a God thing indeed!

At its peak, FBC Leesburg regularly had fifty to a hundred people show up for visitation on Monday afternoon. Eventually, the church averaged three hundred baptisms per year for an entire decade and baptized more than seven thousand people in Roesel's thirty-year pastorate. The church grew by transformation not by transfer. Still, everyone knew that Roesel wanted to start intentionally reaching the destitute.

After Roesel had preached on *ministry evangelism* for five years, his ideas gained traction. Others in the congregation caught the vision. The members dreamed about beginning and doing *ministry evangelism* in the church's neighborhood in houses of various states of disrepair. By the time Roesel retired in 2006, the church had purchased thirty-one parcels of land including twenty-eight houses, built the Ministry Village, the First Academy Leesburg, the Roesel Ministry Training Center, and the Family Life Center without incurring any debt.

The people of FBC Leesburg caught the vision, and God blessed in tremendous ways. Through these ministries, Roesel led his congregation to care for the needs of the poor and destitute while sharing the gospel, thus honoring God's commands in passages such as Matthew 25:31-46. Readers should not think, however, that the remaining twenty-six years of

Roesel's ministry held no opposition to his vision. Voices of opposition arose from time to time. As illustrated in some of the summaries below, Roesel's pastorate proved the need for strong leadership – especially when caring for the poor over an extended period of time.

Rescue Mission

Church members decided to provide a place where homeless people could eat, spend a few nights, and go on their way. So, they opened The Men's Residence in 1982. The facilities were not in good condition. "If the termites had quit holding hands, they would have collapsed," Roesel said of the buildings. The church learned a lot from that ministry. Humble beginnings or not, the church had caught the vision for *ministry evangelism*, and God blessed their efforts. Since then, The Men's Residence has become a long-term discipleship program that houses more than thirty men at a time.

Most men entering the program have drug or alcohol problems, and many suffered some kind of abuse in childhood. The director of The Men's Residence, Jay Walsh, said of that ministry, "It takes broken, empty men who have lost their sense of dignity, and we hope they find the dignity that God wants them to have through Christ." The curriculum deals with these issues.

Today, FBC Leesburg Senior Pastor Cliff Lea and volunteers take time out of their schedules to invest in the lives of these men. Ministry participants attend Bible study six to seven hours per day, four days a week, attend Sunday services, and provide the "muscle" for jobs around the church as needed. Success rates can be tricky in the *ministry evangelism* field, but more than half the men who complete the program leave with long-term sobriety. Even more important, the program has seen innumerable men come to Christ, some of them becoming Christian leaders.

There were growing pains to be sure. Some people didn't like the element that the ministries attracted, and let the pastor know about it in no uncertain terms. "One fellow said, 'I don't think my wife and children should have to walk past that kind of people when they go to church,'" Roesel recalls. "They left, and so did some others. But many more people came than left." The Men's Residence became the first major *ministry evangelism* effort of FBC Leesburg, and God used it to shape the congregation into a caring body of believers.

In the past twenty-seven years, the Children's Shelter Home has served almost three thousand children.

Children's Shelter Home

Again and again, God confirmed Roesel's desire to reach abused and hurting children in tangible ways. Within a few years of doing *ministry evangelism*, a couple in the community donated $25,000 to FBC Leesburg to start a children's home because their own church had liability concerns. Later, a bank offered $35,000 that was designated for a children's home. Pastor Roesel was a grateful receiver of the funds which totaled $60,000 before the project even began. With this funding, the church opened their facility for children in 1985. Lee and Gail Evans moved their two children into one of the houses near the church and offered shelter to children who had been removed from parental custody by the state.

In the past twenty-seven years, the Children's Shelter Home has served almost three thousand children. The home averages between fourteen and sixteen occupants every night and is paid for by a contract with the Florida Department of Children and Families. That contract explicitly states that the children may participate in all the activities of First Baptist, Leesburg, including Sunday school, AWANA, youth camp, and other activities.

Hundreds of children have heard the gospel and accepted Jesus Christ as Lord and Savior through the Children's Shelter Home.

Bob Buford toured once and said to the anchor parent, "Tell me a story."

The home mother responded, "I'll tell you a story. We had two brothers come to our home; one was nine, the other was eleven. They had been so abused and neglected they did not know what a restroom was. They just went wherever they were. They did not use utensils at the table; they just grabbed the food with their hands. When we tried to hug them, they trembled with terror. But the most shocking thing was after the first night when we went to get them up, we could not find them. The bed had not been touched. We found them curled up together in the closet. The Children's Shelter Home has been loving them to normalcy." These stories of restoration – loving children to normalcy – became the pattern for the people of First Baptist.

Pregnancy Care Center

Many ministries were birthed as God spoke to lay people. Roesel felt his calling was not to birth ministries but to fan the flames in the hearts of those who care.

He recalled, "A lady told me that I preached strong against abortion, but talk was cheap. Then she donated five thousand dollars to begin our Pregnancy Care Center. We live in a nation where statistically you have a better chance of surviving on death row than in a mother's womb, so yes, talk is cheap." Through this lady's inspiration, the church began caring for mothers during their pregnancies.

Roesel was advised not to put the church's name on the pregnancy ministry or locate it on church grounds. "That's immoral and deceptive. It will be on our grounds, and it will have our name on it. We are not in the deception business," he said.

"We started out seeing one hundred and twenty every month. We had eleven-year-old girls coming in who were pregnant."

The impact of the pregnancy ministry was immediate and deep. "The greatest sermon ever preached at this church on Sanctity of Life Sunday was not by me, but by a pastor and his wife who held the twins who had been rescued through the Pregnancy Care Center and that they had adopted. That picture was worth many more than a thousand words."

In 2012 alone, thirty-seven abortion-minded young women chose life for their child after coming to the Center. The Center is led by Wanda Kohn who, because of incredible leadership, received the Daniel of the Year Award.

Women's Care Center

The Women's Care Center opened in 1989 as a mirror image to The Men's Residence. That ministry serves a maximum of eighteen women and was the backdrop for the church's 1996 film *The Touch*. Describing the Center, Carol Barber, past director of the Women's Care Center, said, "Most of the women come from an exploitation world and a self-destructive lifestyle that has taken away dignity and self-respect. They are beaten down, but they clean up, and their self-worth blossoms, and their countenance changes – gradually!"[1]

Most women come to the Center with multiple issues and resistance to being helped. The Center interviews prospective residents and must be somewhat selective; they select women who appear ready for change, but they are not staffed to help women with extreme mental illness. They develop a case plan for each woman; then a woman must be working her plan to stay. The women are aware that a church supports the Center, "so we represent God to them. How they perceive me influences how

---

1 George G. Hunter, *Radical Outreach: The Recovery of Apostolic Ministry and Evangelism* (Nashville: Abingdon Press, 2003), 161.

they see God." Barber says, "If they experience unconditional love from us, it is much more than they are used to." They must experience "tough love, with consequences. We allow them to fail in a safe environment. We pick them up, forgive them, and support them, and they learn to move on."[2]

The Center has developed useful guidelines for the ministry of evangelism with this population:

- Don't assume a woman's lifestyle, behavior, or speech signals unresponsiveness to the gospel. Conduct or appearance may be calculated to intimidate or give an air of self-sufficiency when, in fact, the individual feels insecure or frightened.

- Volunteers are encouraged to prayerfully discern when a teachable moment is present.

- Volunteers are to modify their presentation of the gospel for each individual's needs.

- Be willing to sow in the client's life, even if you don't see the person come to faith in Jesus. You may be one of a chain of people whom God will use to draw her to Himself.

- Trust God to convict people and give them faith and life.[3]

Medical Clinic

George Hunter wrote, "Several years later with the help of a hospital grant, First Baptist Church started a three-thousand-square-foot medical clinic for people without medical insurance or payment for medical services and who do not qualify for Medicare or Medicaid. Both patients and medical personnel have become Christians through this ministry."[4] About ninety physicians and fifty other volunteers (nurses, paramedical,

---

2 Hunter, *Radical Outreach*, 161.

3 Hunter, *Radical Outreach*, 162-163.

4 Hunter, *Radical Outreach*, 155.

and clerical people) have served about six hundred patients per month. An expansion of the facility permits the clinic to serve potentially eight hundred to nine hundred people per month. The medical center dispensed over one million dollars of medicine each year, which was generously provided by the pharmaceutical companies. Dr. Vesser was used of the Lord to recruit the doctors.

Daystar

Pastor Roesel led a revival in an affluent community in Atlanta when the local pastor said, "We don't have these kinds of folk in our church field. What can we do?" He went home, prayed about it, and felt led to start a ministry for the "up and out" – a school of fine arts.

In less than two months, over two hundred had enrolled.

In less than two months, over two hundred had enrolled. George Hunter wrote, "Since 1997, the Daystar Academy of Music and Performing Arts has targeted Leesburg's most 'talented' children and youth. Under the direction of Ali Dickson, a vocalist and music educator, a part-time faculty of eighteen mentored over two hundred and fifty children and youth in voice, dance, theater, piano, trumpet, violin, guitar, saxophone, drums, and a range of other instruments, performing arts, and visual arts."

Ali Dickson reported that Daystar Academy proposes "to build a fine arts program that will help students develop their skills to the glory of God. We strive to present positive Christian alternatives that convey the message of the gospel and enhance the climate for evangelism. With the Academy, First Baptist joins a promising evangelical movement to produce people who can communicate with pre-Christian people through the arts."[5]

---

5 Hunter, *Radical Outreach*, 155.

First Academy Leesburg

For many years, Roesel preached that people should view the public schools as a mission field, and he believes that people who are in the public schools in any way, shape, or form should make a difference for Christ where they are. But God gave him a burden in the early 1990s for a Christian school in Leesburg. Not everyone agreed with him when it was started. One lady brought him an enormous bottle of Tums and said, "You're going to need these when you see how much trouble this school will be."

"I never needed one of them," he said.

Today, the existence of First Academy is a testimony of God's faithfulness and willingness to honor the vision He has given Pastor Roesel, despite opposition. The school needed to be academically excellent and unashamedly Christian, so they hired Greg Frescoln to be the headmaster. God has enabled Frescoln to establish First Academy as a fully accredited K-12 school where children can learn the skills to succeed in life and where they can meet Jesus Christ and come to know Him in a personal way.

The faculty is made up of active believers in Christ. The administrators are Christians and the board of directors all put Jesus first. Students attend chapel services where they hear the gospel, and our dynamic minister of music, Stephen Wolgamott, teaches music to the children.

The results speak for themselves. The graduates have gone on to prestigious universities, distinguished themselves in various careers, and some have gone into ministry. More than 80 percent of our student families do not attend First Baptist Leesburg, but they all hear the gospel as a part of the students' curriculum and are faithfully taught God's Word.

Counseling Ministries

When a congregation becomes known as "the Church that Cares," many wonderful things happen, but how do you help all the folks who come to you? The pastoral staff was in danger of being overwhelmed by the needs of the community. At the same time, the church had many people who wanted to help but lacked the training to give pastoral counseling. People Helpers grew from this need. Currently, the church has professional counselors who volunteer to help people in need and teach lay people who desire to help those in need with the basics of Christian counseling.

The People Helpers program, led by Dave and Edna Orser, offers many weeks of intensive classroom instruction on biblical counseling as well as sessions watching a seasoned counselor interact with someone in need. Many of the People Helpers' clients are court-ordered to seek counseling for anger management or domestic violence or other issues. Because the church is using volunteers, the services are free, which is attractive to the clients. Because the volunteers are Christians, they never fail to let the clients know that Jesus is the ultimate answer. This ministry became a key effort in the community for caring for the destitute with counseling needs.

Good Samaritan Inn

Helping enough people catch the vision that the ministry continues once the pastor has left is the real challenge. Charles Roesel retired from the pastorate in 2006. For almost twenty years, Art Ayris served alongside Pastor Charles and learned about *ministry evangelism* and leadership. As the economic crisis of 2008 began to take a toll on the church and ministries' finances, Ayris led the Christian Care Center board in prayer for God's help with finances. And to the surprise of the board, he prayed for guidance in considering the purchase of the Big Bass Motel.

The eighteen-room motel had been a thorn in the side of those trying to help people move from chemical dependency to following Christ at the Christian Care Center. Drugs, prostitution, fights, and every other kind of villainy occurred at the Big Bass Motel.

Within days of that prayer, Ayris negotiated the purchase of the Big Bass Motel which adjoined the Christian Care Center property. The idea was to turn it into a shelter for families who had been displaced because of the economic downturn. The families had to be homeless with no current substance abuse or criminal issues. Their rental payment was that they adhere to a case plan they helped craft, which would address the barriers that led to their homelessness. The program has no set time restriction, but the average stay is six to twelve months.

Many residents and residents' children have accepted Christ for the first time as a result of the ministry.

Transforming the Big Bass Motel into the Good Samaritan Inn presented challenges. It cost more and took longer than expected, which is a general rule in construction. The community was supportive and came together in an extraordinary way. At a recent work day, forty-five people from fourteen different churches volunteered electrical, plumbing, painting, and other skills to help the less fortunate. The program has generated local, regional, and national attention.

In the first eighteen months of operations, thirty adults and forty-five children transitioned from homelessness to economic self-sufficiency. Clients have their own "pastor" in Chester Wood, a deacon at FBC Leesburg. They are required to make appropriate life choices based on the contents of the Scriptures and hear the gospel during their interaction with

Samaritan Inn and Christian Care Center staff. Many residents and residents' children have accepted Christ for the first time as a result of the ministry.

At-Risk Youth Ministry (The Genesis Center)

Years ago, Roesel heard about Saturday Sunday school. The name didn't make much sense – if it was on Saturday, call it Saturday school. If it was on Sunday, call it Sunday school. But be that as it may, he loved the idea of busing upwards of four hundred children to the church campus every Saturday for Bible instruction and fun. The children reached in that ministry were often from rough parts of town, and many did not have fathers at home. The dedicated bus ministry volunteers who transported them and taught them the Word of God were the best, and were sometimes the only positive male role models they had. God blessed that ministry for many years through the faithful service of dozens of volunteers.

Eventually God moved the heart of the community-outreach pastor, Ken Scrubbs, to change direction. Through a godly couple, God made it possible to buy the campus of a Baptist church across the street. He supplied the funds to renovate the campus which housed an after-school program.

Today, one hundred and fifty children receive tutoring, mentoring, and after-school fun through the Genesis Center. Pastor Scrubbs baptizes about thirty children a year through the program and impacts every family. It's quite a deal to walk through Leesburg with Pastor Scrubbs because everybody seems to know him. What's more, he knows them, and God has made Himself known to them through the Genesis Center. Ken Scrubbs received the Governor's Mentor of the Year Award for his outstanding work in the Genesis Center program. The state is considering the use of his program with at-risk children as a model for the entire state.

IT'S A GOD THING

Thrift Store

The Christian Care Center, organized in 1985, is like many non-profits in that it needs consistent revenue streams. In 2006, the first thrift store opened in downtown Leesburg. However, the location was too small, and parking was impossible. In March 2011, the Christian Care Center board of directors and FBC Leesburg agreed to open a larger thrift store in June 2011. It thrives under the able leadership of Gary Gray. Initial income projections ranged from zero to $10,000 per month. By mid-2013, it became clear that the store would generate closer to $80,000 per month. In addition to the revenue, volunteers at the thrift store found they were meeting people from the community who would never darken the door of a church. They came looking for a bargain and left having heard an encouraging word about Jesus and an invitation to join the body of Christ in worship.

The World of Media

But God was not done with First Baptist, the Ministry Village, or the Christian Care Center. Hundreds of churches, ministries, and governmental leaders turned to First Baptist, Leesburg for advice on impacting their communities through ministry-based evangelism. People came from all over the country and the world to see what God had accomplished. Pastor Roesel, Pastor Ayris, and others saw the need for a video to capture the heart and soul of this story. What was conceived as a documentary evolved into the full-length motion picture, *The Touch*. This movie won several film festival awards including Best Feature Independent Film Festival, Best Feature Christian Agape, Best Feature Angel Awards, and Best Feature Florida Motion Picture and Television.

SAT-7, a dynamic television ministry in the Middle East, translated the film into Arabic, Farsi, and Turkish and shows it on their satellite network. Leaders believed it was essential for both believers and non-believers to hear this message of Christian love and redemption. The film was also translated into Portuguese and Hakka Chinese and enjoyed several national network airings. (The film can be ordered by calling the church office at 352-787-1005.)

The church's television program, *The Church Triumphant*, was the flagship program for over twenty-five years on the largest Christian television network in Florida – SuperChannel 55. Tens of thousands of people became acquainted with Dr. Roesel and the ministries of First Baptist, Leesburg through this program.

Because the program was carried live, the church provided telephone counselors each Sunday. One lady kept calling and asking for prayer. She was believing God for saving her son. Year after year, the team prayed for Cecil Johnson. This same Cecil Johnson was eventually reached for Christ through The Men's Residence and became a vibrant witness for Christ.

Christian Graphic Novels

Roesel's executive pastor and right-hand man for many years, Art Ayris, credits the ministry training from Roesel for launching a successful media company. Ayris said, "Under Pastor Charles and in this church, I learned how to raise and manage money, build teams of people and a strong ministry work ethic, and I learned the utmost priority and critical importance of evangelism." Ayris's company, Kingstone Media, rose to become one of the top faith-based comic book and biblical worldview graphic novel companies in the world. A New York Times bestselling author penned a sterling graphic novel titled *Eternity*, which provides a compelling message about heaven and hell.

Conclusion

People still look at First Baptist Leesburg as the leader in ministry-based evangelism and Roesel was esteemed with the Distinguished Service Award in 2000. Receiving this expression of recognition from the Southern Baptist Convention has caused him to consider why God picked him. He says, "God wanted the most ordinary place and the most ordinary pastor in order that people will know without a doubt that it's a God thing. Never forget – any old place will do if God is in the place, and any old preacher will do if God is in the preacher. It's not the place, not the preacher, but God! I say again, it's a God thing!"

– Samuel Smith and Tim Mims

The Great Misunderstanding

———————— ∽ ————————

It will work in large churches, but not in small ones." So goes the common response when people talk about *ministry evangelism*. I believe it is a great misunderstanding that only large churches are able to do *ministry evangelism* effectively. The truth is *ministry evangelism* is a bullet that will fit any gun. Any church, regardless of how small, can do it.

Ministry evangelism is the most effective way of reaching people for Jesus Christ. It displays and proclaims the love of Christ like no other form of caring. The smallest church, Sunday school class, small group, or individual family can reach out through this type of ministry. The story of God's work through First Baptist Church Leesburg describes fully developed ministry structures, but ministry evangelism starts in the heart of one individual who is willing to extend themselves in helping another individual in the name of Jesus.

As you care for people's felt needs and share Christ with them, God will use you. He will use you to change lives, affect families, and impact entire communities. *Ministry evangelism* is a passion for the lost and a way for the church to care for people's deepest needs – needs that are physical, emotional, and spiritual.

People are in need of experiencing the love of God through the lives of followers of Jesus, His church. Walking alongside those in need, building ongoing relationships; providing aid, friendship, and mentoring; and explaining God's mercy and grace are the key components of *ministry evangelism*.

In the Appendix there is a list of over one hundred ministry ideas, most of which can be done by the smallest church. My own story shows that God will provide what you need in order to care for people. Whether yours is a church of fifteen or fifteen hundred, you have what your community needs: the message and the love of Jesus Christ.

> *Little wonder the back door is as large as the front door.*

The foreword, written by Samuel Smith and Tim Mimms, offers an historical sketch of my ministry and focuses on what God did through His people at First Baptist Church, Leesburg, Florida. Chapter One will describe to readers my primary concerns – the "social gospel" and evangelism. Chapter Two lays a biblical understanding of *ministry evangelism* and why we should commit ourselves to it. Chapter Three addresses my concern about winning people to Christ but leaving them in a state of spiritual infancy. Little wonder the back door is as large as the front door. Churches must disciple new believers and not fail to help them grow in their faith. In Chapter Four, I address one of the essential issues in *ministry evangelism*: pastoral leadership. Pastors must lead their people to care for others and share the gospel. Chapter Five explores the issue of finances and *ministry evangelism*. If a church is going to be effective in this ministry, its finances and those of its members must be healthy. Finally, I included an appendix that lists Scriptures to ponder when considering *ministry evangelism*. The Bible should guide a church's ministry from beginning to end.

Testimonies abound of people who found relief from their distress and found Jesus through our words. As an example of what *ministry evangelism* can accomplish, I would like to share the testimony of a woman who received loving care through our ministry in Leesburg, Florida. As we love people through *ministry evangelism*, their lives are changed. Here is one example:

Dear Pastor Roesel,

Recently I was able to tell Louise Gibbs how our family was ministered to by the Pregnancy Crisis Center several years ago. When she asked me if I was willing to write out my testimony for you, I gladly agreed. I wanted to share a beautiful picture with you, but my daughter, who wanted to thank you too, asked to remain anonymous so that her son will never know his life was in question.

We came to Leesburg in January of 1988 as visitors from Niagara Falls. I am a Christian, but at that time my heart was crushed and grieving. Just before Christmas, I had learned that my lovely fourteen-year-old daughter was pregnant by her steady boyfriend. I had been divorced for three difficult years and was working full-time to provide for my two daughters and myself. I knew there was no hope that I could take responsibility for her baby. I knew the risk to her young body if she were to carry a child and the damage to her future if she were to raise her child alone and poor. I could see the "reasonableness" of ending her pregnancy.

We were, for several months, planning to fly down to visit my parents in Leesburg, a trip they planned and paid for as a gift to us. The trip could hardly be cancelled, and I needed my vacation time to decide what to do, so we went. While in Leesburg, I found the Center in the yellow pages and made an appointment for my family to have counseling, with some misgivings, as I had no idea of your philosophy and services.

At the Center, we were shown a film with James Dobson about the processes used for abortion and also about single mothers who chose to keep their babies. A lady gave us literature and told us about the many Christian parents who were eager to adopt.

She gave my daughter a small plastic replica of a fetus about the size of the one growing in her body. I went away less certain that abortion was right for my daughter. Later I was to learn from my daughter that she wanted to keep her baby even if her boyfriend chose not to marry her. I didn't know if I could forego charges against him because it was a case of statutory rape, but she pleaded with me not to, once we had filed a paternity suit.

We were able to enroll my daughter in a new type of school in Niagara Falls, "The Center for Young Parents," where she did an excellent job in the ninth grade. Meanwhile, the boy's father offered to help them get married in Alabama because they were too young for New York state law. He also wanted to provide a home for them with him. I agreed to the marriage, which then took place in late March. Four months later, we all rejoiced as she gave birth to a perfect baby boy.

Today my bright, handsome grandson is six years old and in first grade. My daughter is a beautiful twenty-one-year-old, wise beyond her years. The family lives in a nearby trailer park, struggling, but happy to have each other, and grateful for the support of all four grandparents. My daughter is at the top of her class, studying to be an LPN after having worked as a nurse's aide for several years. Her husband has finished two years of college.

May God bless you as you continue on such a far-reaching ministry.

– A Mother in New York

I hope this book will encourage you and your church to consider engaging in *ministry evangelism*. This type of ministry is about loving God and loving people created in His image. As ambassadors of Jesus Christ, God calls us to live out our love for Him by proclaiming the gospel and serving through good deeds.

The Great Danger

The Social Gospel Avoided

———————— ∽ ————————

What's the problem? Isn't caring for people and their needs a good work? But that is what creates the problem – caring without sharing. One reason evangelicals are hesitant to engage in *ministry evangelism* is the result of the "social gospel." With good reason, God's people fear falling into the trap that believers followed one hundred years ago. By understanding the social gospel movement, we can press toward what God has called us to do: care for people's needs while sharing the gospel with them.

The Social Gospel Avoided

Understandably, evangelicals look on social action without evangelism with suspicion. Social action alone does not meet a person's deepest needs. Christians should support and participate in community efforts to meet needs and confront problems like hunger and homelessness. But the church's business goes deeper. As Christians, we are to feed the hungry, shelter the homeless, and protect the innocent. This expression of God's love draws people to the gospel such that they will come to know Him as Savior and Lord. Our caring ministry must be unconditional, but it must always carry the gospel message.[6]

The apostle Paul addressed our ministry responsibility in these words: *All this is from God, who reconciled us to himself through Christ and gave us the ministry of reconciliation* (2 Corinthians 5:18). Those of us who have been reconciled to God (saved) have been given a ministry. This ministry is the ministry of reconciliation. The question is, "What does it mean to be a minister of reconciliation?"

Findley B. Edge points out that many Christians have related reconciliation only to saving souls; therefore, the one focus of the Christian's ministry is evangelism or soul winning. This view, according to Edge, adopts the Greek dualistic view of human life that sees a person as a body and a soul. It tends to emphasize the importance of the spiritual but gives little attention to the physical.

A more biblical view sees a person as a unit and is concerned with the physical, emotional, social, and spiritual aspects of life. God is concerned with the totality of a person's life; therefore, reconciliation involves the total person and all of his relationships and circumstances.[7]

William Pinson speaks about the need to include the whole person in our ministry efforts. "Not only are we to minister to all people, but we are to minister to all needs. Jesus fixed His ministry on whole people, not on bodies as some medical technicians might, nor on minds as some educators do, nor on emotions as some counselors and psychiatrists do, nor on

---

6 This paragraph, along with the following seven paragraphs, is reproduced from Donald A. Atkinson and Charles Roesel, *Meeting Needs Sharing Christ: Ministry Evangelism in Today's New Testament Church* (Nashville: LifeWay Press, 1995), 107-109.

7 Findley B. Edge, "The Meaning of Ministry," in *LAOS: All the People of God,* eds. Fisher Humphreys and Thomas A. Kinchen (New Orleans: New Orleans Baptist Theological Seminary, 1984), 70.

souls as some religionists do. He was concerned about whole people."[8] Reconciliation brings people into relationship with God by ministering to every area of their lives.

Part of our role in bringing God's redemptive love to others is influencing the structures of society that are detrimental to humanity's well-being. Christians must work to make conditions better for others, especially the downtrodden and powerless. We can accomplish this by becoming involved in both Christian social action and Christian social ministry. Christian social ministry refers to deeds of love and kindness that meet individual needs, such as feeding the hungry, clothing the ragged, and ministering to the sick and imprisoned. On the other hand, Christian social action refers to the efforts of God's people to make needed changes in society to alleviate conditions that hurt others, especially the poor and underclass.[9] Christians must not only minister to people's hurts and brokenness but also seek to eliminate the evils in society that create pain, poverty, and suffering.

Christians must not only minister to people's hurts and brokenness but also seek to eliminate the evils in society.

Delos Miles uses the story of the Good Samaritan in Luke 10:25-37 to illustrate the difference between Christian social ministry and Christian social action. The Samaritan engaged in social ministry by binding the beaten man's wounds and spending time and money to save his life. "If he had sought to change the conditions which led to the Jericho road robbery and mugging, that would have been social action."[10]

Many believers and churches were involved in social action

---

8 William Pinson, "Ministry Now," in *LAOS: All the People of God,* 111.

9 Delos Miles, "Church Social Work and Evangelism as Partners," in *Evangelism in the 21st Century,* ed. Thom S. Rainer (Wheaton: Harold Shaw Publishers, 1989), 55.

10 Ibid.

in the 1960s and 1970s to bring racial justice to a segregated nation. In this current decade, Christians have taken stands on societal issues such as abortion, legalized gambling, crime, and drug trafficking. More attention needs to be given to social justice in areas such as housing, nutrition, and medical care.

Christians should be passionate about the causes they believe in, but the church's witness is negated when Christians become shrill, hateful, and violent. Christians must not let themselves be led to extremism, hatred, and violence. As we attack society's injustices that damage people, we must do so in the spirit of our Lord – the spirit of redemptive love. Our agenda, like that of Jesus, is to do God's work in the world. This means involvement in caring for people's needs and hurts in order to introduce them to Jesus, the Great Physician.

An Ever-Present Danger

The reason people like the term *ministry evangelism* is simple: it avoids being confused with the old "social gospel." That program was a failure because it was all social and no gospel. The greatest danger of *ministry evangelism* is that it is so satisfying when we feel blessed by helping the hurting with their physical needs that we fail to meet their deepest need – a saving encounter with Jesus Christ. We must be intentional in evangelism. We must remember a key fact: the social gospel remains an ever-present danger.

When Jesus said, *Follow me, and I will make you fishers of men* (Matthew 4:19 NKJV), He meant: *Follow me* – that is the command – *and I will make you fishers of men* – that is the promise. If we are following Jesus, we will be fishers of men. If we are not fishers of men, we are not following Jesus.

In Matthew 28:19-20, Jesus gave a command: *Go and make disciples of all nations . . . and surely I am with you always, to the very end of the age.* He also said we would have power: *But you will receive power when the Holy Spirit comes on you; and you will be my witnesses in Jerusalem, and in all Judea and Samaria, and to the ends of the earth* (Acts 1:8). This statement shows that Christian witnessing is not voluntary or mandatory as much as it is inevitable. If Jesus is in my heart, He'll be in my talk. If He is not in my talk, He is not reigning in my heart.

The early Christians took Jesus at His word. They were not trained theologians, but men who still had the smell of fish on their sandals. The women's hands spoke more of goat hair and mutton than the silks of Damascus. But these uncouth folks caused the bystanders to marvel when they saw that they had been with Jesus. The Bible tells us they prayed for ten days. Peter preached for ten minutes, and three thousand souls were saved, and then five thousand. The Lord added daily to their number. The number of the disciples multiplied. Remember what happened from there: Jesus went up, the Holy Spirit came down, Christians went out, the lost came in, and the church continued to grow. What God did with the early Christians, He can do with us today. The power is no less, the purpose no different. It is obvious we have failed to do it His way, and we are not winning the world. We are losing the world.

We do not truly love people if we do not tell them about Jesus. The twentieth century's great atrocity was not Hitler murdering six million Jews, as horrendous as that was. It was not Stalin murdering twenty million of his own people, as shocking as that is. It was not Americans murdering untold millions of unborn babies, as staggering as that is and continues to be. The greatest atrocity of the twentieth century is that two billion people on the earth have never heard the gospel a single time because we have made the gospel the greatest story never told. The two most embarrassing questions you can ask a Southern Baptist congregation are: "How long has it been since you brought someone to Jesus Christ?" and "How long has it been since you even tried?"

In general, we are in danger of not being evangelistic at all. This danger becomes worse when ministering to the poor and forgetting the Lord's command to share the gospel. It is at this point that Christians fall prey to the ever-present danger of the social gospel.

Illustration: The Wall

We are now a denomination in which 25 percent of our churches are baptizing nobody. Another 25 percent are baptizing three or fewer per year. That means half the churches in the self-proclaimed most evangelistic denomination on the planet are reaching three or fewer. According to our best numbers, a church burns through thirty-four thousand dollars per convert saved. Is a soul worth it? Of course. But with the same thirty-four thousand dollars we should reach dozens of people for Christ.

Think about this for a moment: If a church of one hundred people were to disciple each member in such a way that each member was to reach one person who followed Christ in baptism in a calendar year, that church would be in the top one-tenth of 1 percent of Southern Baptist churches for the year. Why are we not all reaching at least one person for Christ every year?

Now I must give this warning: Winning people to Christ is not just a matter of following a formula. It is good to learn from the great men who have given us FAITH (Forgiveness, Available, Impossible, Turn, Heaven), EE (Evangelism Explosion), and CWT (Continuing Witness Training). I heartily recommend these tools. But at the same time, we must learn to be spontaneous with a witness born in a moment of opportunity. In my time of ministry, I have seen God use many different ways to draw people to Himself. In my own life, one instance often comes to mind.

In this particular event, I went to a Baptist Assembly ground to teach a conference on personal evangelism. As I pulled up to the building, I noticed there was a postal service worker delivering the day's collection of mail. I recognized the gentleman delivering the mail as one of the deacons from First Baptist, Leesburg whose name was Red. Red has always been an affable fellow, and he was teasing back and forth with a mountain of a man. This guy was probably six-foot six-inches tall, three hundred pounds, with not an ounce of fat.

"You ought not to tease Red; he's a good man," I said to the fellow.

The man looked back at me with fire in his eyes. He was a black man and took umbrage at my calling Red a good man, but not him.

Why are we not all reaching at least one person for Christ every year?

"Don't you think I'm a good man?" he said slowly and forcefully.

At this point, the conversation could have gone any number of ways. But, thanks be to God, it turned to the only thing that really matters, Jesus Christ.

"I don't know if you're a good man or not," I said. "The only good thing about Red is that Jesus is in him. Is Jesus in you?"

He looked at me puzzled and said with genuine interest, "No, Jesus is not in me."

"Well, then there's nothing good in you."

Ten minutes later, that man kneeled down right where we were and accepted Jesus as his personal savior. A few weeks later, he was baptized and became a very active, productive member of the body of Christ. The great tragedy is that although he had worked on that property for several years, by his own admission, no one had ever shared Christ with him.

Like the priest and the Levite, we are sometimes so busy being religious that we don't take time to be godly. The hardest part of having a spiritual conversation with someone is bringing up the subject. Once we are willing to be obedient and talk to people about Jesus, we'll find that the conversation we dreaded becomes easier than we ever expected.

First Kings 20:38-40 is a warning that is very applicable here, a passage that reveals one of the primary reasons we are not reaching the world: *Then the prophet went and stood by the road waiting for the king. He disguised himself with his headband down over his eyes. As the king passed by, the prophet called out to him, "Your servant went into the thick of the battle, and someone came to me with a captive and said, 'Guard this man. If he is missing, it will be your life for his life, or you must pay a talent of silver.' While your servant was busy here and there, the man disappeared."*

"That is your sentence," the king of Israel said. "You have pronounced it yourself." Then the prophet quickly removed the headband from his eyes, and the king of Israel recognized him as one of the prophets. He said to the king, "This is what the Lord says: 'You have set free a man I had determined should die. Therefore it is your life for his life, your people for his people.'"

Here we have a story of a man who has one thing needful, one thing important, and one thing primary to do for the Lord. But while he is busy here and there, doing what pleased himself, the one thing needful, primary, and important is neglected. He neglected the important task and gave his first-class loyalties to third-class causes. He was defeated by secondary successes.

This is a temptation we all wrestle with. The temptation is to spend our lives doing good things to the exclusion of the best. But how do we know what is best? The answer is simple. What are we doing that will matter a million years from today? Most of the stuff will not matter next month. But if we bring someone to a saving knowledge of Jesus Christ, we have accomplished something for all eternity.

Or to put it another way, what is the only thing I can do better here than in glory? It's not praise. Certainly praise is important. But in glory, I will have one of the greatest voices because the Bible says the last shall be first. It is not prayer. And to be sure, prayer is vital. We can do more than pray after we pray, but we cannot do more until we pray. But on the other side, I will be able to talk to Him face to face. It is not purity, because in glory we will all be perfect. The only thing I can do better here than on the other side is tell a lost person about Jesus Christ. The urgency makes it the priority. In this life, we have a very limited amount of time.

> *I have only just a minute.*
> *Just sixty seconds in it.*
> *Forced upon me – can't refuse it.*
> *Didn't seek it, didn't choose it.*
> *I must suffer if I lose it,*
> *Give account if I abuse it.*
> *Just a tiny little minute,*
> *But eternity is in it.*
> *It needs to count for His glory.*
> (Author unknown)

Most of us will be busy doing something. But if we are not careful, and we stay busy doing a lot of good stuff, we will not have time for that which is best.

Remember that the king was not condemned because of iniquity. He was condemned because of what he failed to do, or the sin of omission. The man was not condemned because of ignorance. He knew he was supposed to guard the prisoner and keep him from escaping.

Likewise, our problem is not that we lack the knowledge of what it is we are to do. There has never been a time when people have had more information. You don't even need to go to the bookstore and pay money for training in how to lead people to Christ. You can get on the Internet and get it for free! But if we have learned anything in the last few years it is this: You don't grow by what you know; you grow as you flesh out what you know.

You don't grow by what you know; you grow as you flesh out what you know.

In this passage, we notice that the man was not condemned because of inability. He had the necessary tools and training. He had all that he needed, except availability. His priorities simply did not match up with his master's. Finally, the man was not condemned because of inactivity. He was not lazy. He was anything except lazy, going here and there.

How many times are we *busy here and there* rather than doing the one thing needful, one thing important, and thus ignoring what God has for us to do? We fail because we did the good to the exclusion of the best. One thing must be the passion of every Christian and considered the number-one task: bringing a lost world to Jesus Christ.

I've had people say, "Well, Pastor, you have the gift of evangelism, and I just don't have that gift." But we all have the responsibility of bringing the lost to a saving knowledge of Jesus Christ. I don't care how many good things we do. I don't care how much time we spend or how busy we may be. If we're not bringing the lost to Jesus, we are not giving first-class loyalty to first-class causes.

What if every Christian in a church took seriously the responsibility of bringing the lost to Jesus? Rather than being a glorified country club that exists for itself while a lost and hurting world dies without Jesus, why don't we spend our time reaching the community for Jesus? I believe our communities would start looking like Jerusalem did not long after Pentecost.

I'll never forget a quote that I read once in a tract, purportedly the words of an atheist. Though it is long, I think it worthy of reprinting here:

> If I firmly believed – as millions say they do – that the knowledge and practice of religion in this life influences the destiny in another, then religion would mean absolutely everything to me.
>
> I would cast away earthly enjoyments as dross, earthly cares as follies, and earthly thoughts and feelings as vanity.
>
> Religion would be my first waking thought and my last image before sleep sank me into unconsciousness.
>
> I should labor in its cause alone. I would take thought for the morrow of eternity alone. I would see one soul gained for heaven worth a life of suffering.
>
> Earthly consequences would never stay my hand or seal my lips. Earth, its joy and its grief, would occupy no moment of my thoughts.
>
> I would strive to look upon eternity alone and on immortal souls around me, soon to be everlastingly happy or everlastingly miserable.
>
> I would go forth to the world and preach to it in season and out of season, and my text would be, "For what will it profit a man if he gains the whole world and forfeits his soul? Or what will a man give in exchange for his soul?" (Matthew 16:26 NASB)

When British athlete C. T. Studd read those words, he knew he had to go beyond formal religion and commit his life to Jesus Christ in a new way. That new way meant giving everything he had to see people come to know Christ. What about us?

Certainly, we face an ever-present danger when ministering to the poor and needy in our cities. We can begin to care for the needs of people around us and never tell them about Jesus. But we should not let the failed social gospel movement keep us from doing what God wants. Christians must be faithful to the Bible's teaching by avoiding the social gospel and embracing *ministry evangelism*.

CHAPTER TWO

The Great Example

Jesus & Ministry Evangelism

———————— ⁓ ————————

Equal to the danger associated with the social gospel is the danger of ignoring passages in the Bible that command Christians to care for the poor and needy. It is sad that many Christians trashed this whole concept rather than correcting the social gospel by making it evangelistic. We avoided caring for people's physical needs lest we be accused of being liberal.

Instead of ignoring biblical passages that call us to care for the poor and oppressed, we should seek to be faithful to God's will. We should hold the ideal that we see in the Bible: caring for other's needs while sharing Christ. Eli Stanley Jones said, "The social gospel divorced from personal salvation is like a body without a soul; the message of personal salvation without a social dimension is like a soul without a body. The former is a corpse. The latter is a ghost."[11] Neither social efforts nor evangelism, when separated from the other, is biblical. But, you say, what right do you have to say that? I say it because the Scriptures say it.

---

11 Thomas S. Rainer, ed., *Evangelism in the 21ˢᵗ Century* (Wheaton: Harold Shaw Publishers, 1989), 19.

Scripture's Call to Ministry Evangelism

> *"When the Son of Man comes in his glory, and all the angels with him, he will sit on his glorious throne. All the nations will be gathered before him, and he will separate the people one from another as a shepherd separates the sheep from the goats. He will put the sheep on his right and the goats on his left.*

> *"Then the King will say to those on his right, 'Come, you who are blessed by my Father; take your inheritance, the kingdom prepared for you since the creation of the world. For I was hungry and you gave me something to eat, I was thirsty and you gave me something to drink, I was a stranger and you invited me in, I needed clothes and you clothed me, I was sick and you looked after me, I was in prison and you came to visit me.'*

> *"Then the righteous will answer him, 'Lord, when did we see you hungry and feed you, or thirsty and give you something to drink? When did we see you a stranger and invite you in, or needing clothes and clothe you? When did we see you sick or in prison and go to visit you?'*

> *"The King will reply, 'Truly I tell you, whatever you did for one of the least of these brothers and sisters of mine, you did for me.'* (Matthew 25:31-40).

I will not comment on all of the Scriptures in Appendix 1, but this particular text in Matthew is the defining Scripture of my life. No passage of Scripture should rouse the church to action on behalf of hurting people more than this text.

When I was in school, I was always concerned about the final. What's going to be on the final? I didn't want to learn anything I didn't have to learn. Those finals were of little importance, but there is one final that really matters. It is called the last judgment, and we already know what's going to be on that final! Our lives will change dramatically when we realize that God's expectations do not simply consist of a list of things not to do, such as not smoking, drinking, cussing, and so on. His expectations involve helping people in need.

Has it ever dawned upon us that every sin mentioned in this Scripture is a sin of omission? The recurring refrain is that people He condemns did nothing wrong. It is that they did nothing. One of the great tragedies is that we do not realize how terrible sins of omission are because they are less violent, less visible, and less condemned by the world. Yet the Lord Jesus emphasized the seriousness of sins of omission over and over and over.

There's a whole lot more said than done. With Jesus, there was more done than said.

Why did Jesus condemn the fig tree in Matthew 21? It's not because it had bad fruit. It's because it had no fruit. Again, why did Jesus condemn the rich man in the parable of him and Lazarus (Luke 16:19-31)? The rich man did not hit Lazarus or curse him or abuse him in any way. He simply did nothing. Likewise, in the parable of the Good Samaritan, Jesus condemns the priest and the Levite because they simply passed him by.

It may be said of this age that we know more and do less than at any other time. At our fingertips, we have a wealth of knowledge. After all is said and done, there's a whole lot more said than done. With Jesus, there was more done than said. He taught more by what He did than what He said. He could have talked about integrity in the workplace; instead, He worked in a carpenter shop. He could have talked about the worth of children; instead, He stopped a sermon to love a child. He could have talked about the worth of women; instead He treated them with respect.

Jesus could have talked about humility; instead He washed

the disciples' feet. He could have talked about the pain of hunger; instead He fed the multitudes. He could have talked about the burden of being blind; instead He gave sight to the blind.

Jesus could have talked about the trouble of being crippled, but he said, "Arise, take up your bed and walk." He could have talked about the challenge of forgiving, but while hanging in humiliation and pain on a cross, He prayed for the people. He could have talked about the willingness to sacrifice for others, but He died on Calvary for you and for me. That's the reason even lost people have a respect for Jesus Christ.

Examples like these continue throughout the New Testament. In many cases, the church ignores the example of Jesus and is guilty of omission – not caring for the poor and destitute according to the Bible's standard. The Bible calls us to serve the lowly while being in a meaningful relationship with them.

Christians love the church. But the world doesn't. The word of many people is Christ, yes, church, no. When the world looks at the church, they see an organization that exists to extract their money to maintain staff, buildings, and programs. But if the world sees a church that is giving, serving, loving, and reaching out, they sit up and take notice. Then they realize that the church is truly about the business of Jesus because that's what He spent His life doing. He was a giver, not a taker.

Matthew 14 tells of Jesus' heart breaking because John had been put to death by Herod. Our Lord needed to get away, but He did not succeed. Many of us would consider the crowd's following Him as a rude interruption. But Jesus saw interruptions as opportunities for service. We know that this was a Southern Baptist crowd: they were hungry. The disciples did what most modern churches do when confronted with the needs of the crowd: They said, "Let's send them away."

That's what we say to the dirty people, the different people, and the deprived. "Let's send them away." But of course, Jesus didn't send them away. He fed all of them, five thousand men, not including women and children. At the end, twelve baskets were left over, one for each disciple as a reminder that God can meet their needs with enough to spare.

As long as a church ministers to hurting people, it will never lack for an audience. Many New Testament passages, such as Romans 12:13 and James 2:14-17, command Christians to care for the needs of their fellow believers. There are hurting people in the body of Christ, and we are to care for our brothers and sisters. But if there is so much hurt in the church, how much more is there in our communities? It is high time that we quit hiding behind the walls of our sanctuaries and get out into the world where the people are. We need to care about them and their hurts and love them, so no matter how low or how dirty or how difficult or how bad, they will know they are welcome in our family. The church, the body of believers, will be the one place where they know somebody wants them, where someone's face lights up when they see them.

Today, confusion arises from the purpose of Jesus' mission to the poor. Most evangelicals would say the "poor" are those who recognize their need for God, or words to that effect. Too often, evangelicals then adopt sub-biblical attitudes toward the poor and refuse to help them in any tangible way. Folks on another part of the ideological spectrum argue that they are in fact economically poor and that practically Jesus' whole mission was to remedy poverty.

Jesus did not suffer from either misconception. He performed miracles of mercy such as healings, miraculous feedings, exorcisms, and even raising the dead. But those actions never became the focus of His ministry. At most, the miracles resulted from Jesus' compassion for those whom He saw in need (Matthew 14:14) and as a way to share the gospel (John 10:38; 14:11). When people tried to force kingship upon Him, Jesus got away from them (John 6:15) because a political program for the relief of poverty was not His focus.

We can take our cue from Jesus' own attitude toward mercy ministry. An element of mercy and compassion should be part

We may never know the impact one loving act of service may have upon the world.

of every Christian's approach to those in need. Too often, modern Christians make much of the Protestant work ethic, which can be misinterpreted to mean everyone should look out for himself or herself. The poor receive little consideration as if each person who is economically indigent is lazy or addicted to drugs or mentally unstable.

The truth of the matter is that many people who live in need do have some of those problems. But God loves them just the same. As Christians, we have an opportunity to help provide for their physical needs. That is not a burden, but a chance to show them the love of Christ in a way that can open the door for God's love to fill them and change their lives. We may never know the impact one loving act of service may have upon the world. We do know that God will use us in tremendous ways if we are faithful to the Bible's command to care for others and tell them about Jesus.

Reflections on the Transfiguration

The transfiguration gives us great insight and helps us understand what it means to be in a meaningful relationship with the poor and lowly. In Mark 9, we see two scenes that apply directly to our own lives – the mountaintop and the valley. Initially, Christ and three of His disciples were on the mountaintop, and how wonderful it was for them.

Like their experience, Christians have times when we are overjoyed by the spiritual exhilaration, the Shekinah glory, praise, worship, and adoration associated with being in God's presence. We are euphoric when the holiness of God quickens our conscience. The beauty of God purges our imagination. The truth of God feeds our mind. The peace of God fills our heart. The purpose of God overtakes our will. It is a foretaste of glory. Little wonder Peter wanted to build three tabernacles and stay right there. People long for that.

Dr. Martin Luther King Jr. delivered his famous speech first to twenty-five thousand in Detroit in June 1963. Two months later, he took it to the Lincoln Memorial, and before two hundred and fifty thousand he said, "I have a dream that one day on the red hills of Georgia, the sons of former slaves and the sons of former slave owners will be able to sit down together at the table of brotherhood." When I served on the Southern Baptist Convention's Executive Board, Gary Frost (now a regional vice president at the North American Mission Board) told me about a Promise Keepers event where forty-eight thousand gathered in Atlanta. Bishop McKenney led in the observance of the Lord's Supper. Black and white gathered at the Lord's Table. What an experience! The mountaintop is a magnificent experience, but all of life does not happen there.

The second scene we see in this passage is the valley. We see an anxious father, a sick son, and frustrated disciples. All Christians go through similar experiences, from mountaintop foretastes of God's glory to the troubles of this life. We go from the sanctuary to the street, from the sublime to the sick, from the bliss of Sunday to the burden of Monday, from the mountaintop to the valley, the Monday-morning blahs. You might be on cloud nine because of the miraculous acts of God on Sunday. Then some negative member catches you and gives you a full dose of carping criticism. He might complain that the music was too loud or that the church should sing more hymns or more contemporary songs.

Or, you might leave a conference excited about some new

ideas, and you discover your church does not share in the excitement. You and your spouse may have a wonderful time away by yourselves and worshipping the Lord for His goodness in your life. When you return from the weekend, the realities of a difficult relationship or another hardship come roaring back to your mind.

A preacher taught an evangelism outline for this text. I invite you to ponder two of his points. First, God does not need people on the mountaintop who are not willing to go into the valley. God has not called us to be what one charismatic preacher referred to as Hallelujah Junkies. Many people go from one service to another trying to experience one emotional high after another.

God does not need people on the mountaintop who are not willing to go into the valley.

They stand on Sunday and raise their hands to the heavens, but on Monday are not willing to reach their hand to the needy. If we truly worship, truly praise, truly love God, it will result in loving service. We cannot worship God faithfully without caring for the lowly in our communities.

God has called us to the valley of the shadow of death, to the valley of the hurting. I never knew how full that valley was until we became involved in *ministry evangelism*. This valley includes the homeless, the lonely, the abused child, the neglected mother, and the unborn child – the very people who need Christ and are crying out for relief from their circumstances. We have what they need; yet many Christians dare to resist the valley. They prefer the security of the sanctuary to the sacrifice of the streets.

God has committed the hurting to our hands. What do we see when we look at our hands? Are they delicate hands – too delicate to deal with the sordid side of life? Are they busy hands – too busy to take time for those in need? Are they dirty hands – too much a part of the problem to be part of the solution? I pray not. I pray that we will have merciful hands, reaching out in the name of Jesus.

The excuses for not ministering are many. Some people claim that saving the lost is not our business, and we should focus on praising God, prayer, study, and fellowship. Others claim that caring for the hungry and the poor is not the business of the church. Did not Jesus say the hungry will always be with us? These excuses also lead some people to disregard the aged, the lonely, the aborted child, the drug addict, and other humans suffering from tremendous oppression and grief.

But I would remind you of Luke 4:18-19: "*The Spirit of the Lord is on me, because he has anointed me to proclaim good news to the poor. He has sent me to proclaim freedom for the prisoners and recovery of sight for the blind, to release the oppressed, to proclaim the year of the Lord's favor.*" In the face of this apathy, Jesus says we are our brother's keepers.

Years ago, I had a fashionable church member who came to me before Thanksgiving. She had a little project on her heart for the less fortunate. "Pastor, I've been talking to my husband, and we know there are a lot of hungry people out there, so we want to buy some turkeys to give to these poor people," she said. "Pastor, I would like you to deliver them for us."

Knowing her, I couldn't let that happen. "No, God wants you to deliver them," I said.

"Oh, pastor," she said. "I just don't feel comfortable with people like that. How 'bout you doin' it?"

I told her, in essence, that if she was a Christian she needed to get comfortable with "people like that" because Jesus is.

People miss blessings from the Lord because they are not willing to pay the price. When Christians are unwilling to leave the mountaintop and minister to people in the valley, they miss an opportunity for the Lord to work in their own lives.

Second, God cannot use the man in the valley who has not

been on the mountaintop. Mark 9:28-29 says, *After Jesus had gone indoors, his disciples asked him privately, "Why couldn't we drive it out?" He replied, "This kind can come out only by prayer."* This involves the Spirit's power, but that power will be present only if we are genuine worshippers of Jesus. We must invest time in worship and prayer. We must experience God on the mountaintop before descending into the valley effectively. No ministry has vitality apart from worship and prayer.

We can and should worship God alone in our quiet time, but it is imperative that we also do it together. Hebrews 10:25 says, *not giving up meeting together, as some are in the habit of doing, but let us encourage one another–and all the more as you see the Day approaching.* When we truly love the Lord, we do not want to forsake the assembling of ourselves together. We do not look for excuses to stay away from God's house with God's people – and believe me, in sixty years of ministry I have heard every excuse that can be offered. Just as there is no vitality in ministry apart from praise, ministry has no vitality apart from the church.

There must be that time alone and time together in the presence of the Lord if we are going to have power in the street. God does not want the man on the mountaintop who is not willing to go into the valley. God cannot use the man in the valley who has not been on the mountaintop.

When the people of God understand and live out these two reflections from the transfiguration, a few things will happen:

1. We will do some new things.

I've been a Southern Baptist for seventy-seven years. I know Southern Baptists, and we don't like change. I often say when we do something, we'd better do it right the first time because we're going to be doing it that way for the next two hundred years. But if we keep doing the same thing the same way, we're going to get the same results, and that's not impressive.

At Leesburg, we instituted Saturday Sunday school. It didn't make any sense at all. I mean, if you're going to have Sunday school, shouldn't you have it on Sunday? So why did we do it? Because it met a need in the community that would not have been met any other way. Hundreds of kids came every week and heard about Jesus when previously they would have only heard the name "Jesus" as a swear word. A church must be willing to be open and try new things. You can't go into the valley and say, "We've never done it this way before." Reaching people in the name of Christ requires both listening in ways we are not accustomed to and trying new things we may have never considered.

2. We will do the old things extremely well.

We go to conferences and hear great preachers tell great stories about their great churches so we decide we must duplicate what they're doing. We decide to throw everything out and start over. Do away with the old and bring in the new. But there are some old things that still work. We just need to do them unusually well. One of these old things is Sunday school. In my opinion, one of the greatest evangelizing and discipling arms of the church is the Sunday school. But we need to do it unusually well.

Consider traditional hymns. Many churches discontinued them because they were being done so poorly. If they had been done well, there would have been little problem. But when someone who looks like they have dead lice falling off them leads a hymn that's supposed to be exciting, it is no wonder they have a problem with it. We must do what we do extremely well. There is a vital place for both traditional and contemporary, but both should be done with excellence.

3. We will use God's resources wisely.

Using God's resources carefully is critical. The sanctuary at First Baptist was built in 1962. We still use this sanctuary. We considered building a new one, but decided we could give more to missions and ministry if we did not. We elected to use the sanctuary four times per Sunday and have four Sunday schools, which works unbelievably well.

Near the end of my term at First Baptist, Leesburg, we raised independent funds to construct a training center with a conference room. That building is used today for Bible fellowship classes, classes for people working with our ministries, meetings for the various community agencies that work with our Christian Care Center, training and classes related to *ministry evangelism*, and more. We never built a building that would serve one purpose and one purpose only.

Few things are more disappointing than churches spending exorbitant amounts of money for a building they only use three hours a week. If you build an enormous building, you should have some kind of idea what you can do with the building on days other than Sunday. I don't believe God will bless a church with more resources until they use the resources they have wisely.

4. We will loose the laity.

Those sitting in our pews are a mighty army for the Lord. They are ready to go to battle. We must loose them, equip them, and empower them to reach the world for Christ. It is sad that in our churches when there's a job to be done, we feel we must hire someone to do it. Our churches are dying from "staff infection."

I made an agreement with the Lord that during the first million years in eternity I would not attend another committee meeting. Then one day I said, "Why wait? I won't do it anymore now." I turned this task over to lay men and women who did a far better job than I could have done, and doing so freed me to do what God had called me to do: to preach, pray, and equip the saints for the ministry.

These wonderful lay people provided the resources necessary to radically multiply our ministry. The greatest mistake I ever made was when I had the idea I was the only one in the church who knew how to do anything. The greatest move I ever made was to loose, equip, and empower lay people to use their gifts to impact the world for Jesus.

> *The greatest mistake I ever made was when I had the idea I was the only one in the church who knew how to do anything.*

I believe that if we are not ministering to hurting people, we are guilty of high treason, criminal neglect, and absolute disobedience. Ministry is not an elective, but rather a required course and a divine mandate. If we will embrace God's call to *ministry evangelism* by caring for people's needs and sharing Christ, we will see Him use us in tremendous ways. What we will see happen is a disciple-making process through *ministry evangelism* like no other approach to evangelism and discipleship.

CHAPTER THREE

The Great Mistake

Not Discipling New Believers

————————— ⟨∞⟩ —————————

Because of God's call in Scripture to *ministry evangelism*, we know that caring for others' needs is not the social gospel. When combined with sharing Christ, caring for people is a biblical, disciple-making process. Some churches short-circuit the way the God would have us help new believers grow in their faith. Love them and leave them, dip them and drop them. One of the great tragedies is that in the most defining moment of a person's life, the moment they receive Christ, we give them about five minutes in a front pew filling out a card.

Little wonder that we lose over 60 percent of those who make decisions for Christ. This problem plagued me personally for several years until it dawned on me that the reason we were losing them is that we did not adequately minister to them in the beginning stages of their walk. As a result of many years of trial and error, I found a plan that works. We virtually closed the back door of our church. The following stages illustrate how churches should help individuals grow in their faith through spiritual development.

Stage One: Initial Discipling

Statistics for the past several years paint a troubling picture. At least one-half of all members of Southern Baptist churches are classified as inactive, meaning that these people have not attended for at least one year. Therefore, only about 50 percent of Southern Baptist church members can be considered active

The command is not to make converts, but to make disciples.

by any definition. When we consider that *active* is defined as "attending a church service once in twelve months," the picture worsens. Obviously, many of these "active" members are not truly involved in the church's life and ministry. In too many churches, the body of Christ cannot function because it is crippled by parts of the body that are inactive.[12]

What has created the problem of uninvolved and inactive church members? A major cause is a misunderstanding of the Great Commission. When Jesus gave this command to His disciples, He said *go and make disciples of all nations* (Matthew 28:19). The command is not to make converts, but to make disciples. The difference between the two is significant. Many churches are effective in making converts, but not very good at making disciples. The experience of trusting in the Lord Jesus Christ for salvation is indispensable. Evangelical Christians believe in the absolute necessity of the salvation experience. But something is wrong with evangelism that does not result in discipleship.

Discipleship describes the ongoing nature of the Christian life. Disciples are followers of Jesus. Disciples are pupils. They are learning, growing, developing believers. Disciples are becoming more like Jesus in love, attitudes, and actions. Disciples are serious Christians who are growing *in the grace and knowledge of our Lord and Savior Jesus Christ* (2 Peter 3:18). Disciples are not perfect, but they are becoming what they were saved to be – vital, functioning parts of the body of Christ.

---

12 This paragraph, along with the following two paragraphs, is reproduced from Atkinson and Roesel, *Meeting Needs, Sharing Christ*, 82-83.

Ultimately, developing a disciple is the Holy Spirit's work, but God's work in the individual's life involves human cooperation. The believer must want to grow and develop in discipleship, and the church must provide opportunities for discipleship. During my years pastoring at First Baptist Church, Leesburg, Florida, the leaders understood the importance of discipleship to *ministry evangelism*. After people committed their lives to Jesus Christ, the church provided tools to help them develop as disciples. Years of experience in *ministry evangelism* made it clear that as a person's relationship with God deepened, that person became more like Christ. We realized that the transition from spiritual infancy to maturity required time, but the process had to begin immediately for a new Christian and had to continue until God shaped the Christian in accordance with His purpose. In my ministry at First Baptist, Leesburg, we identified seven steps that we believed to be essential in properly discipling new Christians:[13]

Step 1: Passionate Invitation

Discipleship begins with the *conviction* that Christ is our only hope, the only way to God, based on John 14:6.

> *Jesus answered, "I am the way and the truth and the life. No one comes to the Father except through me."*

It burns with *compassion* according to Romans 9:3.

> *For I could wish that I myself were cursed and cut off from Christ for the sake of my people, those of my own race.*

It is bold because of the sterling *character* of the pastor. If there is compromise in our lives, there will be complacency in the invitation. Deuteronomy 11:1 says:

---

13 In addition to these seven steps, find some helpful ideas of disciple making in Atkinson and Roesel, *Meeting Needs, Sharing Christ*, 87-88.

Love the Lord your God and keep his requirements,
his decrees, his laws and his commands always.

It is beautiful in *clarity*. When we use phrases like "The doors of the church are open," we fail to communicate clearly. The lost man might say, "Great – I can get out of here," which is not what we want to see happen. So, pastors must explain and simplify their words to convey what they are asking.

It is born through claiming the lost of Jesus through times of *prayer*.

Effective disciple making will exhibit these characteristics through a passionate invitation. It was my practice several times each year to have all the deacons come forward and form a line across the front of the church. I would then ask my people, "How many of you have a lost friend, relative, or acquaintance you're concerned about? If you do, I want you to come forward and mention the name of the person to one of our deacons. Do not give any detail. Don't say, 'I'm concerned about John, I've known him for twenty years, etc.' Just say, 'John.' God knows the circumstances. Don't come unless you're also willing to say I'm going to pray daily for this person, and I will seek in the next two weeks to share Jesus with him or her."

Hundreds come forward when we do this. We then pray for all the people who have been mentioned and for those who came forward that they would have the opportunity to bear witness.

This practice does several things. It makes people aware that they have lost friends and family in their lives, which is something we tend to forget. Also, I found that my church members would commit to pray daily for this person when we did this in our church.

Another result of this practice is that it helps church members seek opportunity to bear witness. After praying for their friends and family, our church members were much more willing to share Jesus with others. All of these things were backed by thoroughly trained counselors and bathed in celebration.

For example, one Sunday morning two little girls came down the aisle. One said to me, "Pastor, this is my best friend. I brought her to Jesus this week." I drew a little circle of people together and had a party celebrating the little girl who brought her friend to Jesus. I shared this with the congregation so they too could celebrate, and told them a celebration was also going on in heaven. Because our people had the conviction that Jesus is the only way to God, they made passionate invitations to people around them to believe in Jesus. God used these passionate invitations to bring many people to Christ during my years as their pastor.

Step 2: Wise Counsel

No period in a Christian's life is more critical than the moments following their decision to believe in Jesus. During my years as a pastor, we had everyone who came down front get thirty minutes of counseling, which required trained counselors. So I trained over one hundred counselors at First Baptist, Leesburg, training them how to lead someone to Christ. While there are many effective ways to share Christ with someone who responds to the pastor's invitation, we found the most effective way was using the old natural – carnal – spiritual person's approach used in many tracts. However, we did not use the actual tract because we found it more effective to draw it out while the people were watching.

We told the person that we were delighted and thrilled he made a decision to believe in Jesus. Then the counselor described three people, and when he finished, he would ask the new Christian which one accurately described him.

When we were in the room with these people and asked them to describe where they were spiritually, the responses surprised us at times. I had more than a few people ask if they can be between an "un-natural" and a "super-natural" Christian. Remember, the question is not, "How do you feel after a really great church service?" but "What is your normal, day-to-day life really like?" You wouldn't believe the number of people who said to me, "You know, I thought I was a Christian, but there has never been a time in my life that I committed my life to Jesus Christ," or "I just grew up in a Christian home and figured I was a Christian."

These conversations did not happen in just a few seconds or down front at the end of a service only. In the course of the various ministries at FBC Leesburg, the majority of our evangelistic opportunities came through our approach to *ministry evangelism*. The staff and volunteers had more time to disciple people when meeting with them on a regular basis. That's why probably 70 percent of the seven thousand baptisms we saw during my time there came about through one of those ministries. Helping individuals determine where they were at spiritually required wise counselors, and wise counselors came through me training them to be prepared.

Step 3: Required New-Members Class

Requiring new believers to go through a new-members class was another important step. We noticed that some people who accepted Jesus and received our counseling did not stick around. I asked my deacons to help "close the back door of the church" to keep our new members on track. They came up with a required New Member's Class, and it was accepted well. Our new members underwent six hours of instruction about the church, what we did, and where they would fit in. New Christians – especially Christians who come to Christ through *ministry evangelism* – need help to understand the church and find their place within the body of Christ. Many people won through *ministry evangelism* do not have a background in church and benefit from new-members classes in tremendous ways.

Step 4: Place of Service

Based on what we discussed in our new-members class, we determined places of service for each one of them. When we introduced the new Christians on Sunday nights, we identified their chosen place of ministry. Naturally, we couldn't have new Christians teaching classes, but there were many ways to get people involved in

There is no such thing as a "nobody" in the kingdom of God.

serving the Lord. We had a plumber who accepted Christ, and his ministry was to keep the plumbing in good repair at the church. Likewise, we had a painter who offered his services. With our ministries, we could always find something that a new Christian could do in serving the Lord – folding clothes at the Benevolence Center, working in the nursery, or some other contribution – everyone had a task and every task had meaning.

We always stressed that there is no such thing as a "nobody" in the kingdom of God. Take my dear friend, Cecil. He came to our men's ministry (The Men's Residence) strung out on drugs, and he insists he was dropped off at the front desk by an angel. I wouldn't argue with him. During my last year as pastor at FBC Leesburg, Cecil led no less than fifty people to Christ. He wasn't counting, but I was. Today, Cecil is a deacon in the church. He works tirelessly with the men in The Men's Residence, preaches all over the Leesburg area, runs his own business, and is still winning people to Jesus Christ.

Step 5: Sunday School Enrollment

For our church, the process of assimilating new members into the church and starting them on the road to becoming mature disciples involved Sunday school. We assigned each new church member to a Sunday school class immediately. The classes – or other forms of small group ministries – are extremely important to *ministry evangelism* and discipleship because a Sunday school class teaches God's Word and ministers in times of physical need. Also, Sunday school classes provide a group of Christian friends for love, encouragement, and support. New Christians are much more likely to develop in discipleship if they become active participants in Sunday school.

Step 6: Sponsor Assignments

It is vital that we have someone stand alongside the newborn Christian for at least one year. Sponsors should call their new brother or sister at least once a week, checking to see how they're doing. They should take them out to eat at least once a month. Also, they should say to them, "Call me anytime; just don't ever say 'I hate to bother you,' because it is never a bother."

We cannot continue in the Christian life alone. Even long-time Christians need other brothers and sisters in the Lord to help them remain faithful. Being a part of the body of Christ should not happen as isolated individuals. The concept of older believers is a great way to encourage new Christians to continue in their newfound faith. Generally, it is best to introduce the new Christian and the sponsor at the final session of the New Members Class.

Step 7: Assimilation Secretary

Overseeing this discipleship requires a leader. An assimilation secretary is a key position in the disciple-making process. The task of assimilating new members does not end with the three-session New Members Class. This person is the one who assigns new members to sponsors. In addition, the assimilation secretary tracks the new members' attendance and calls them periodically during the first year of membership. If the situation requires further attention, the assimilation secretary assigns visits from a deacon, a Sunday school teacher, or a staff member.

Stage Two: Equipping for Service

As churches help Christians follow these seven steps, they will become more and more useful for kingdom service. Not only do we need to disciple the young Christians, but we need to train them specifically for the task they are gifted to perform. Too often

It is not enough to help people get off drugs and into sub- sidized housing.

we know a little bit about everything, but are not trained in the area of our specific callings – a jack-of-all-trades and master of none. Toward the end of my ministry, I was developing a program to require new workers to be certified in their area of service before they were allowed to serve.

Stage Three: Equipping Graduates of the Programs

When people graduated from one of our *ministry evangelism* programs, we did not think it was enough that they be "in recovery" forever. Too often, that's just trading one addiction for another. When we looked at people, we hoped to see God restore them in every way: in their relationship to God, in their relationships to their families, in finding a place of service in a local church, in their usefulness to their fellow man, and in their capacity to work and provide for themselves and those they love. It was not enough to help people get off drugs and into subsidized housing on government assistance for the rest of their lives. That was a secular approach that sees less poten- tial in people because of their past while we believed that God would have us focus on their future.

Good examples of this approach come from our Men's

Residence program and the church's Women's Care Center. Our Men's Residence program was four months long. After those four months of intensive Bible study, counseling, efforts at family reunification, and help with physical problems when appropriate, men graduated to the service phase. For a month, we had a time of guided Bible study, volunteer work, and discernment of where God would have these men serve in the body of Christ.

Our Women's Care Center program was very similar, except that the first stage is six months long. There was no special reason for the difference; it was just our experience that the women benefit from a little bit longer time.

In his book *Radical Outreach*, George Hunter offered several helpful insights to our ministry at FBC Leesburg. He wrote:

"The church's body of insights gained from this ministry would be useful to many churches and many ministries. The Center teaches all volunteers five guidelines for engaging in useful ministry with this population.

- Help a woman identify her options; do not decide for her what she should do.
- Help a woman determine the steps she should take; do not take the steps for her.
- Help a woman discover her own strength; do not rescue her and leave her still vulnerable.
- Help a woman take responsibility for her life; do not take responsibility for her.
- Help a woman find a new life in Christ; do not try to reform the old life.

Volunteers and staff have to reinforce persistently the principle of the client's personal responsibility. While we provide temporary relief to women in crisis, we must not make relief the permanent response. The primary goal is to share our lives, our time, our skills, our energy, and the gospel in ways that empower clients to break out of the cycle of sin and destitution, and to be free to assume responsibility for their own needs."[14]

Ministry evangelism involves much more than handing out things that people need. It leads people to become what God would have them to be: worshippers and workers for His glory. To become effective in ministry, we found several relational qualities to be essential for a new Christian's ability to be used by God:

Empathy involves the sensitivity and skill to "think with" and "feel with" the other person, to communicate back to the woman what she is thinking and feeling, and thereby to experience identification with her.

Genuineness involves appropriate honesty, transparency, openness, and vulnerability; it helps create the friendship that is more transformative than a mere professional/client relationship.

Unconditional acceptance means "to affirm and care for the person, apart from her lifestyle – not condoning the woman's sinful behavior, but accepting her in spite of it."

Humility is "the ability to recognize your own limits as well as strengths." The need for humility applies not only to staff and volunteers, but also to the whole ministry. Humility involves not presuming to offer services for which God has not provided the human and financial resources, and not feeling guilty for the services you cannot provide. The Women's Care Center, for instance, desired to offer psychiatric therapy within its ministries, but could not.[15]

We found that our men and women brought with them the mentality prevalent in our society that work is about getting

---

14 Hunter, *Radical Outreach*, 162.

15 This list is found in Hunter, *Radical Outreach*, 163. Hunter offered these summary statements of our commitments to relationship qualities necessary for effective volunteer ministry.

rich and serving oneself. By having them do some volunteer work at our Benevolence Center or our Thrift Store or in some other part of what we do, we tried to help them to see that God wants each person to *work, doing something useful with their own hands, that they may have something to share with those in need* (Ephesians 4:28). We understand the Christian life to be one of service, and work involves both the labor that brings in money and the labor that brings people into the kingdom of God.

For this reason, we worked with the men and women to establish a kingdom mentality and help them discover what their gifts and talents were for serving the kingdom of God within the church. This allowed them to meet their own financial obligations and provide a testimony to God's grace in their lives through honest hard work.

We had numerous men from our Men's Residence eventually become pastors, music ministers, youth ministers, deacons, Sunday school teachers, and other servants. We must give first credit to God. But the gentle, humble work of servants like Joann McCall, Jay Walsh, and Dave Fleming was instrumental in helping these men see themselves as God saw them. When we met the needs of people in our community, led them to Christ, and equipped them for ministry, we saw God restore lives and empower people to change our city.

CHAPTER FOUR

The Great Challenge

Pastors with Passionate Leadership

——————————— ⌒∞⌒ ———————————

A movement rises or falls on leadership. Ralph Waldo Emerson said, "Every great institution is the lengthened shadow of a single man. His character determines the character of the organization." The success of *ministry evangelism* depends on pastoral leadership with a passion for the hurting. Six leadership characteristics are essential if we are to be successful.

Devout Faith

Andy Anderson once said to me, "Charles, do you realize that the modern church could do almost everything it is doing, even if God didn't exist?" We are not alone when it comes to weak faith. I think of Jesus' feeding of the four thousand as recounted in Mark 8. We read in verse 8 that four thousand men, not counting women and children, *ate and were satisfied.* I believe they were not only satisfied with the food they ate, but with the presence they enjoyed. Jesus had fed them with seven loaves and a few fish.

Remember, Jesus had already fed five thousand. They had forgotten those experiences because they were filled with doubt. They again wondered how the situation would be handled. Like them, we go from miracle to miracle, but at the same time, we wonder if God can handle the next situation. The disciples still worried in Mark 8:17-21. Despite the miraculous feedings of five thousand and four thousand, they worried because they had brought only one loaf of bread into the boat with them. Jesus was totally exasperated with them:

> *"Why are you talking about having no bread? Do you still not see or understand? Are your hearts hardened? Do you have eyes but fail to see, and ears but fail to hear? And don't you remember? When I broke the five loaves for the five thousand, how many basketfuls of pieces did you pick up?"*

> *"Twelve," they replied.*

> *"And when I broke the seven loaves for the four thousand, how many basketfuls of pieces of did you pick up?"*

> *They answered, "Seven."*

> *He said to them, "Do you still not understand?"*

Too many pastors see magnificent opportunities as impossible challenges. What does it take to convince us that our God is able? For all He asks, we have all that He is, and that is all it takes. If God is the God of miracles and if we believe the first verse in the Bible is true, then anything is possible. Good leaders must have a devout faith.

Deep Compassion

We forget to pray "our" and instead pray, "God bless me, my wife, son John, his wife, us four, no more." We cannot reach a world until our love includes the people loved by God. Great pastoral leaders show deep compassion through several ways.

First, they love dirty people.

These are not the people we usually want to associate with. We don't want that kind of people. We want the respectable people, the influential people. But let me remind you: Jesus did not hobnob with the snobs or elect the elite. In fact, He was criticized for hanging around with the wrong kinds of people.

One story that stands out in my mind describes the transition "from the mire to the choir." While I was pastor at Leesburg, an elderly lady stood to sing. I had heard her sing many times, but I had never heard her testimony. During that service, she felt moved of the Lord to share her testimony.

"When I was a young girl, I was sexually molested by my father," she said. "I married early to get out of that horrible situation, and I married badly. It ended in divorce. After that, I went to the streets, and for many years, I sold my body. Then I met Jesus face to face, and He cleansed my life and made me a trophy of grace."

> *I will never grow tired of hearing of God's grace or cease to rejoice when He changes someone's life.*

She then sang in the fine, fashionable First Baptist Church of Leesburg. When she finished, the people gave her one of the longest standing ovations I could remember in the history of the church. People there celebrate the saving grace of Jesus Christ.

We live in an age in which people are jaded. Some folks don't like to hear the stories about God bringing people from the mire to the choir. To those people I can only say, "I will never grow tired of hearing of God's grace or cease to rejoice when He changes someone's life."

Second, they love different people.
A little girl with Down syndrome got on a plane. A missionary sat down beside her. She nudged him with her elbow and asked, "Do you brush your teeth?"

And he replied, "Yeah!"

She said, "That's good, because if you don't, your teeth will rot out." She nudged him again and asked, "Do you take a bath?"

He replied, "Yeah!"

She said, "That's good, because if you don't, you get germs and die." She nudged him a third time and asked, "Do you love Jesus?"

He replied, "Yeah!"

She said, "That's good, because if you don't, you go to hell."

About that time, a man sat down beside the missionary. Another nudge and her question was: "Ask him; ask him, does he brush his teeth?"

The missionary did, and the man replied, "Yeah."

Second nudge. "Ask him; ask him, does he take a bath?"

The missionary did, and the man replied, "Yeah."

Third nudge. "Ask him; ask him, does he love Jesus?"

"No, I don't," he said. "I'm going through a terrible time, and I've been thinking about talking to someone about Him." The missionary brought the man to a saving knowledge of Jesus, but I don't think he would have if it hadn't been for that precious little girl with Down syndrome who used her giftedness to glorify Jesus.

Third, they love diseased people.

In New Testament times, leprosy was the problem. Today, it is AIDS. I heard a pastor reminiscing about the early days of the AIDS epidemic. We had some crazy ideas back then about that disease: that it could jump fifteen feet from person to person and other strange ideas. The pastor was walking back to his office between services when a young man came up and asked for a word with him. The pastor said he was very busy and he would only be able to talk while they walked back to his office.

"Here's what I need to tell you," the young man said. "I have AIDS."

The pastor grabbed the young man and hugged him. Then

he walked into his office, closed the door and cried out, "God! What have I done?"

He said God told him, "You didn't do anything; I did."

Fourth, they love those who are deprived.
These are not only the people who lack food and clothing and shelter, but also the people who are emotionally deprived. Nobody cares about them. Nobody calls. They are so lonely they sit in a home waiting to die. They could be dead for a week, and no one would know or care they are dead.

I received a phone call from a lady who refused to tell me who she was. "The last pastor I called hung up when I wouldn't tell him my name," she said. "Are you going to hang up?"

"I promise I won't hang up on you," I replied.

We talked for less than five minutes, and before she hung up, she asked, "Pastor, would it be all right if I were to call you again?"

"Absolutely. No problem at all," I replied. "Any time you want to." The only thing the woman wanted was a friendly voice because she had no one to talk to.

There are more people like these in your community than you know. That's the reason we began a ministry reaching four hundred shut-ins a week.

Once, a lady told me that on Thanksgiving she went into her mobile home, shut the door, and pulled the shades because she was so miserable and lonely. For many years after that, we hosted a Thanksgiving dinner at my ranch for everyone who had nowhere to go. Stop and think for a moment about the people in your own life: the widow grieving the loss of her husband of forty-five years; the awkward teenager with acne who is never chosen but is shunned by the "acceptable" crowd; the newcomer separated from old friends; the defenseless, unwanted little child who is shuffled from one foster home to another.

IT'S A GOD THING

They are a part of your life for a reason. Our privilege in being a part of the body of Christ is to provide a loving fellowship, dispelling loneliness. People need to know they are loved, and if there is any place where that ought to be a reality, it should be in the body of Christ.

Fifth, they love those who are disappointing.

When I was at Stetson University, the chaplain told of a little boy who accepted Christ on Sunday night. Monday morning, he saw the young man sitting on the sidewalk and asked him how he felt about the decision he made the night before.

"Best *bleep* decision I ever made," the little boy said. Somebody then tried to tell the chaplain that the little boy had not been saved. He had been, but he hadn't learned how to talk like a Christian yet. This little boy didn't need someone to tell him he wasn't saved after all. All he needed was some loving guidance.

> *If we want people to love us as we are, we must love them as they are.*

Sixth, they love those who are difficult.

If we want people to love us as we are, we must love them as they are. An old couple expressed the tension that we live in when dealing with difficult people: "To dwell there above with those that we love, oh, that will be glory. To live here below with those that we know, that's another story."

I have found that many times troubling people are troubled people. Usually it's not even you that they are upset with. They are just full up to the brim with anger and resentment, and you happened to be in the way when they came along. Often, the best way to love difficult people is to reflect on how difficult you can be because all of us have been at one time or another. If we want to be loved when we are difficult, we must love people who are difficult toward us.

By now, you realize that the "right kind of people" are the

people with whom we deal every day. The idea is not to create a community of like-minded folks who all act, dress, think, and feel the same way. We want to bring God's love and His grace and His kindness to the people we come into contact with every day. That, my friends, will amaze people on the outside as much as anything else we do. As we see God changing our hearts toward "unwanted" people, He will drive us to attempt great things with the confident hope that He will complete that which He brought to our minds to do.

Decisive Humility

Our words should not be "serve us," but "service." Traveling across North America to lead at conferences, I was first surprised and then pleased to discover some of the greatest leaders in our convention are marked by humility. I led in a revival at FBC Dallas, and had the privilege of spending time with Dr. W. A. Criswell and hearing wonderful stories about his ministry.

One moving story was of a mentally challenged man who would take up much of Dr. Criswell's time every Sunday at the door while others were waiting to be greeted. One Sunday, a staff member saw the man headed for Dr. Criswell. He took him by the arm and gently escorted him around Dr. Criswell and out the door. Dr. Criswell saw this and the next morning called the staff member into his office. He said, "I saw what you did yesterday. Don't ever let me see you do that again. I'm probably the only man who gives him undivided attention each week. That is important to me." That is true greatness.

Determined Persistence

One of my favorite historical personalities is Winston Churchill. On one occasion, he was addressing his alma mater. He had a long manuscript prepared, but as he looked out on the sea of faces, he put the manuscript aside. He then spoke these words:

"Never give up, never give up, never, never, never give up." And he sat down. These words ring in my heart. To be sure, many times we're tempted to throw in the towel, give up, quit, and walk away. But we need to be able to say at the end of our lives, "It is finished." God help us to finish well.

A page of John Wesley's diary reads as follows:

Sunday a.m., May 5:
Preached in St. Ann's. Was asked not to come back anymore.

Sunday p.m., May 5:
Preached at St. John's. Deacons said, "Get out and stay out."

Sunday a.m., May 12:
Preached at St. Jude's. Can't go back there either.

Sunday p.m., May 23:
Preached at St. George's. Kicked out again.

Sunday a.m., May 19:
Preached at St. Somebody Else's. Deacons called special meeting and said I couldn't return.

Sunday a.m., May 26:
Preached in meadow. Chased out of meadow as a bull was turned loose during the service.

Sunday a.m., June 2:
Preached at the edge of town. Kicked off the highway.

Sunday p.m., June 2:
Afternoon service, preached in a pasture. Ten thousand people came to hear me.

Little wonder he shook the world!

Delightful Cooperation

I read that the giant redwood trees grow only on the West Coast of America and no other place on this earth. Most of the trees have burn and char scars, recalling past difficulties. Some have huge caverns carved out of their middles by gutting fires – some so large that two or three people can stand inside. But the trees still grow, so full of life they can't be killed, and that makes all the scars seem unimportant. One tree towers 308 feet over us. That's more than thirty stories tall! It's been alive for fourteen hundred years. It's as if one day God said, "I think I'll build a tree. Who cares if it takes five hundred years or a thousand or whatever. I just want a tree. Who's counting?"

So what is the secret of the redwood? How can it last so long and endure so much? Unlike the palm tree whose taproot goes down into the ground as deep as the tree is tall (thirty feet up, thirty feet down), the redwood has no taproot at all. That's why you never see a redwood standing alone. Never. They are always in clusters, groups, and groves. The might of the tree is not in itself. Here is its strength: For every foot in height, the redwood tree sends its roots, not down, but three times that distance – out! That's right, out! If the tree is three hundred feet tall, its roots go nine hundred feet out, intertwining with all the groping roots from the other redwoods in the grove. By the time a few thousand years go by, those fellowshipping roots are so woven together, there is no way a tree could fall down. It is held up by the strength of its brothers and sisters.

We stand strong when we stand together. It breaks my heart when I see my fellow Southern Baptist pastors who are independent, having little or nothing to do with their associations or state or national conventions.

I learned the heartbreaking news of our precious grandson Andrew's death at 8:00 in the morning. By 9:00 a.m., we had received calls from all over America. I thank God for the loving support of my fellow pastors. I don't know how I could be as effective without them. Pastors who lead well are committed to delightful cooperation.

Dynamic Energy

It is the last of these that I feel compelled to dwell on. Temple care is a silent issue in many of our churches. From one's initial introduction to the Lord Jesus, we learn that He always talks in totals. That is, total commitment of the total person to the total purpose of the Lord Jesus. I believe in a fivefold surrender: Mind (Intelligence), Heart (Love), Will (Obedience), Spirit (Dynamic), and Body (Usefulness).

That last one seems to be the glaring omission in Christian commitment today. I heard a preacher say that Christians are enraged against certain sins – and we should be. But many Christians seem to be blind to sins against the body. Why are our health insurance premiums so high if we don't drink or smoke? The reason is, we are otherwise irresponsible when it comes to total temple care. If caring for our bodies were nothing more than an act of vanity, I wouldn't waste a section of this book on it. But Scripture reveals God's concern about our physical well-being. In Genesis 2:7 we find: *Then the LORD God formed a man from the dust of the ground and breathed into his nostrils the breath of life, and the man became a living being.* Then He smoothed the rough edges off man and created woman. The human body is no fluke of evolution's process. It is God's design and handiwork, His masterpiece.

Why did God give us these incredible bodies? So we can use them to honor Him. First Corinthians 6:19-20 says, *Do you not know that your bodies are temples of the Holy Spirit, who is in you, whom you have received from God? You are not your own; you were bought at a price. Therefore honor God with your bodies.* We don't own our bodies. In fact, Paul calls honoring our bodies an act of worship. *Therefore, I urge you brothers and sisters, in view of God's mercy, to offer your bodies as a living sacrifice, holy and pleasing to God – this is your true and proper worship* (Romans 12:1).

T-E-M-P-L-E Care Involves Six Essentials

(T) Testing

Several years ago we were getting ready to go to the Holy Land. Edna Sue, my wife, had an appointment for a mammogram and said to me, "I think I'll just wait until we get back from the Holy Land – I don't think I have a problem."

I said, "That is something you don't wait on because you never know." When she came home from the test, she said they found a little problem. I immediately called a friend who is an insider and asked her for the scoop.

She said, "Pastor, I wept when I saw it. It is not only cancer; it's a most aggressive kind of cancer." After a lumpectomy, chemotherapy, and radiation, she is still cancer-free after eleven years. Praise God! Prior to the test, she had no indication of having breast cancer and could not even feel the lump after they'd found it with the

A lot of food is looking to go into the ministry.

mammogram. Had we not had the test, I would have lost my wife. There is so much we don't know if we don't have regular checkups. I'm told the reason that women live much longer than men is that they have enough sense to have regular checkups, and men do not.

(E) Eating

We lose over one million people per year to food-related diseases. The rounding of America is one of our most serious health problems, especially with pastors. A lot of food is looking to go into the ministry. The list of best-selling books always has two or three dieting books on it. "More die in the United States of too much food than of too little," observes one doctor. Three enemies we need to watch: sugar, fat, and salt.

(M) Mental Attitude

One pastor suggested that our environment seems to be stress free. Our babies seldom die, and famine is virtually unknown to us. We have telephones when we get lonely, air conditioners when we get hot, aspirin when we have a headache, and TV when we get bored. And yet, we live in an age characterized by depression. We have suicide, suicide gesturing, personality disorders, obsessive behaviors, eating disorders, panic attacks, alcohol and other drug abuse, phobias, and psychoses.

I've read that over the last decade, the number of therapists has risen tenfold. We have more mental workers in the United States than we have police. Mental health beds are filled to capacity. Spending for mental health has increased 100 percent in the last five years. One-third of that spending is for psychiatric illness. Forty percent of us will be in psychotherapy at some point in our lives. In six years, psychiatric hospitalization for adolescents tripled. One-half the people in hospitals are there because of psychosomatic problems. We are told that our inability to cope with stress causes many of the illnesses from which we suffer and die: peptic ulcers, high blood pressure, certain strokes, migraines, asthma, muscle spasms, even dandruff. Stress depresses the body's immune system.

Three enemies exist at this point. First, many pastors *worry*. For years I had to deal with this. I earned my Ph.D. in worry. I used to worry so much that when I was not worrying, I worried because I wasn't. I always felt worse, and I felt best because I knew how bad I was going to feel when I felt bad again. I finally realized that we worry because we aren't placing our faith in the Lord. Not only that, most of what we worry about will never happen.

Deuteronomy 31:6 says, *Be strong and courageous. Do not be afraid or terrified because of them, for the* LORD *your God goes with you; He will never leave you nor forsake you.* Isaiah 41:10 states: *So do not fear, for I am with you; do not be dismayed, for I am your God. I will strengthen you and help you; I will uphold you with my righteous right hand.* God does not want us to give in when battling anxiety.

Second, many pastors struggle with *guilt.* One of our great problems is that we proclaim God's forgiveness and believe He has forgiven us, but we cannot forgive ourselves. We need to realize that we are all sinners saved by grace, and the only time God is pictured as running in the Bible is when He is running to forgive (Luke 15). The only thing God forgets is confessed sin. If God is willing to do this, we certainly need to forgive ourselves. First John 1:9 tells us, *If we confess our sins, he is faithful and just and will forgive us our sins and purify us from all unrighteousness.*

Finally, pastors struggle with boredom at times. We forget that in Christ we have a new relationship to God, a new regard for others, a new reason for living, and a new restfulness concerning the beyond. We need to remind ourselves of this daily, that life should always be lived to its fullest.

(P) Poison

I realize that this does not apply to most pastors, but as we lead others, these are issues we must address. Pastors must be prepared to address tobacco and alcohol abuse among their people. God's people need to think through the poisons they put into their bodies, and pastors must lead them to avoid anything that will harm the body God has given them.

(L) Leisure

You've heard it said, "Come apart and rest awhile – or come apart." If it is so important that God made it one of the Ten Commandments, we need to take rest seriously.

(E) Exercise

Exercise is key to the health of God's people. It will promote general health and well-being, sharpen the mind, lower the percentage of body fat, help achieve proper weight, insure cardiovascular conditioning, lower blood pressure, reduce stress, and help prevent some forms of cancer.

Conclusion

Pastors need to be great leaders when guiding God's people to engage in *ministry evangelism*. Keeping these characteristics of a good leader in mind, a pastor can stay on track to help his church be a merciful and evangelistic congregation. The people of God look to him, and he needs to help them by exhibiting and developing with his church members several key traits of godliness: devout faith, deep compassion, decisive humility, determined persistence, delightful cooperation, and dynamic energy.

CHAPTER FIVE

The Great Assurance

Money & Ministry Evangelism

------------∽------------

When thinking through *ministry evangelism* and getting involved as a church, the first question often asked is, "Can we afford it?" That is the wrong question. The question should be, "Is it God's will?" And if it's God's will, He can afford it. He owns the hills, the cattle on the hills, the taters in the hills. He owns it all. An old saying goes, "Salvation is free, but ministry costs money." So where did First Baptist Church, Leesburg find all of the money it takes to operate its ministries? It was found when God moved the hearts of His people to give.

FBC Leesburg & Money

Not long after we opened the Women's Care Center, God spoke to me. He didn't speak to me audibly as He does to some, but it was the strongest leading I've ever had in my life. The Lord said, "It's not right to put these people up in a shack." The church had just raised two million dollars for the Family Life Center, and the local economy had been decimated with two citrus freezes. I was undeterred because I learned from Elijah that a god who cannot burn wet wood is no good. You don't have to have ideal circumstances. So I announced to the church what God had laid on my heart.

A lady came up to me who was not a member of the church

and said, "I have a little piece of land I'd like to donate." I thought she was talking about a lot. She was talking about *a lot*. The plot of land was forty acres that appraised for $825,000. She also wanted to make a cash donation of $100,000. She went to her house and retrieved the cash from its shaving-kit hiding place.

One Wednesday night, another couple from the community asked to see an outline of the building locations, which an architect had already made of what would be called the Ministry Village. If you have a vision, it's important to put it in a form that people can see. The husband looked at the wife and said, "What do you think?"

She said, "Let's do it." That couple, who were not members of our church, gave us $75,000. People continued coming out of the woodwork as momentum built to bring the Ministry Village into existence.

A man in the church who was so shy that most people could not call him by name asked me one question, "Is it going to be first class?" I told him it would be nicer than anything my wife and I had lived in up to this point in our lives, so yes, it was going to be first class. He gave $100,000.

Rather than contact fundraising professionals, I told the church the Holy Spirit was raising the money. I said, "Let's not interfere with what He's doing. If God leads you to make a pledge, bring it to the altar on the last Sunday of the month." At the end of the month, counting everything we brought in to that point, we had two million dollars committed for the village.

But the work was not done. The demand for the Children's Shelter Home had grown so great that I saw a need for a second children's home. The church had enough money to begin a second home, but not complete it. I stood up in the first service and told them we needed $100,000 for a second children's home. They laughed, but I didn't. After the second service, a godly couple from Gainesville, Georgia, who were not members of the church, came to me and said they believed God wanted them to give $100,000 for the second children's home. (We don't ever say if you're not a member, we don't expect you to give.)

The community had begun to take notice of what was going on at First Baptist Church. The local hospital in Leesburg approached me with a proposal to provide a nurse and liability insurance for the Ministry Village. All we had to do was provide the space. That was a no-brainer. Later, they called and said they had a lot of money they needed to give away. I told them they certainly knew how to call the right man. They built a state-of-the-art medical facility on our campus.

The financial aspects of the clinic's success have not outstripped God's miraculous provision.

The partnership between FBC Leesburg and the Central Florida Health Alliance is today called the Community Medical Care Center (CMCC) and provides free medical care to thousands of clients every year. Today, the hospital and the Lake County Health Department provide hundreds of thousands of dollars in funding. More than ninety doctors, both retired and actively practicing, volunteer their time. The doctors include cardiologists, orthopedic surgeons, general surgeons, pulmonologists, and many other specialists. Other doctors who do not actively serve at the clinic help many clients for free as a result of referrals and favors to those who serve on the front lines.

The clients at the CMCC cannot have any other kind of insurance: no Medicare, Medicaid, or private insurance. These are the people who would otherwise fall through the cracks and end up in the emergency room with a fever or a cold. Volunteers at the CMCC come from dozens of churches and share the love of Christ with these people when they are most receptive to it. The CMCC has also launched a long-term chronic disease program that helps people with diabetes learn how to manage their treatment.

The financial aspects of the clinic's success have not outstripped God's miraculous provision. A few years after it opened, the current director of the CMCC went to speak at a Presbyterian church seeking a dentist to help clients. She didn't find one; she found eleven. Today, more than four hundred people per month receive free dental care at the clinic.

FBC Leesburg continued to expand into other areas of *ministry evangelism*. A church across the street was dying and offered to sell its facilities for $250,000, even though it was valued at approximately three million dollars. As has happened so many times before, a man from the church wrote a check for the entire amount. Today that church facility is home to the Genesis Center, an after-school program that reaches roughly one hundred and fifty at-risk youths every week with spiritual guidance, academic help, and structure.

Pastor Ken Scrubbs runs the ministry and enforces a balanced set of values. "When they come in here, they know they are in a church," he said. "We expect them to respect the facilities and each other, but we work hard to make it a fun place with the best in technology and the best help they can get as far as their schoolwork goes. We hire licensed teachers to help them. We want for them to have a positive impression of church, to learn to love God and respect each other, and to introduce them to Jesus Christ."

Churches often refuse to get involved in *ministry evangelism* for fear of not having enough funds or the threat of lawsuits. Our ministry testimony disproves both excuses. In addition to all of the miraculous fundraising, the Christian Care Center has never once been sued in its existence.

Christian Financial Freedom & Money

If we want people to freely give, we must teach them how to freely live. We must teach them the principle of financial freedom. This principle has four implications for all Christians that pastors must teach their people.

First, we must teach our people to think like Christians.
We are to love God, love people, and use money – not use God, use people, and love money. First Timothy 6:6 says, *But godliness with contentment is great gain.* Lowell (Bud) Paxton made millions of dollars with his creative idea for the Home Shopping Network on television. But Bud Paxton's life was not at peace. There was a troubled marriage and a multitude of frustrations in his life.

Then Bud became a Christian, and his whole value system was realigned. People now mattered more than things, eternity more than time. On October 19, 1987, Paxton was scheduled to address the International Convention of Stockbrokers in Washington D.C., a gathering of eighteen hundred stockbrokers or representatives of brokerage firms. But when he entered the room at 1:30 p.m., only about twenty people were there.

> *I'm just thankful that my trust isn't in the things of this world.*

Earlier in the day, the stock market had started to plunge – a plunge that would go 508 points. The people in the room had panicked. Everybody left. Paxton said that as he walked down the hallway of his Washington hotel, he soon quit counting the number of businessmen in expensive three-piece suits who were crying their eyes out because their lives were crumbling and their security was threatened. Paxton himself lost over a hundred million dollars on the stock market that day. His preacher asked him, "Aren't you really ruffled? How do you feel?"

He said, "I'm just thankful that my trust isn't in the things of this world." What a great word! What a great faith! We need to be careful because money is dangerous. It should be labeled "Handle With Care." It beckons us, woos us, tantalizes us, and seduces us. We devote the best years of our lives to it. We glory in accumulating it and lie awake at night figuring out how to stockpile more of it.

Matthew 6:24 says, *No one can serve two masters. Either you will hate the one and love the other, or you will be devoted to the one and despise the other. You cannot serve both God and money.* Also, think about Mark 10:23: *Jesus looked around and said to his disciples, "How hard it is for the rich to enter the kingdom of God!"* Finally, Luke 12:15 offers a helpful reminder: *Then he said to them, "Watch out! Be on your guard against all kinds of greed; life does not consist in an abundance of possessions."* Remember the truth we see in Scripture concerning seeking material wealth: *For what shall it profit a man, if he shall gain the whole world, and lose his own soul* (Mark 8:36 KJV). Thinking through these texts will help us think like a Christian.

Second, we must teach our people to work like a Christian. Scripture is clear that we are to work. For example, Proverbs 14:23 states: *All hard work brings a profit, but mere talk leads only to poverty.* Or, we could look to Proverbs 10:4: *Lazy hands make for poverty, but diligent hands bring wealth.* Another passage is Proverbs 12:24, which says, *Diligent hands will rule, but laziness ends in forced labor.* Romans 12:11 encourages us in this way: *Never be lacking in zeal, but keep your spiritual fervor, serving the Lord.* First Timothy 6:10 is another key text: *For the love of money is a root of all kinds of evil.* What can we do?

One leader suggested that first, we need to have the right *attitude.* For some people, work is a curse or a sentence to be served. They endure the five-day workweek to support the activities of a workless weekend. They lie awake at night scheming ways to arrange early retirement. Meanwhile, they are bitter, feeling their best years of life will be wasted in work. For others, work is celebration, a joy, and a privilege.

What makes the difference? The difference is found in a person's attitude. We ought to thank God for the privilege and opportunity of work. We ought to thank Him for the privilege of the being a witness in the workplace.

Second, we need to have the right *aptitude*. The greatest knowledge a person can have is to know God and to know God's will for his life. Work is your joy if it is what God has called you to do. Thinking through God's will for us is closely tied to a person's aptitude. Consider a few questions when determining if you have the right aptitude for a particular line of work: Have I studied it scripturally? Have I prayed it through? Have I observed the doors opening naturally? Have I sought counsel? Have I waited on the Lord? Have I received peace? Does it glorify God?

Finally, we must have the right *gratitude*. We need to be thankful for the privilege of having work to do, and, as Christians, we need to express that gratitude to our employer. Without the right gratitude, one's work will not glorify the Lord. Pastors must help their people develop a right attitude toward work that will align with their right aptitude carried out with the right gratitude. Then, God's children will work like Christians.

Third, we must teach our people to spend like a Christian.
For some reason, most pastors do not address this subject. Think about it. If at the end of the month a person is presented with an opportunity to use money for evangelism, but must make a car payment or a house payment, what do you think he will do? It is not what we earn, but what we do with what we earn that makes the difference. If your outgo exceeds your income, your upkeep will be your downfall.

We live in a world of people who buy things they don't need, with money they don't have, to impress people they don't like. Many people need to have plastic surgery – they need to cut up their credit cards because they don't have the discipline to properly use them. Christians also need to avoid *impulse buying*. They should sleep on it and think it through to determine whether they need a certain product and whether they can afford it.

> We are happy with our house until our best friend gets a new one, and all of a sudden ours is a shack.

Avoiding *envy buying* is important as well. We are happy with our car until our best friend gets a new one, and all of a sudden ours is a rattletrap. We are happy with our house until our best friend gets a new one, and all of a sudden ours is a shack. We need to avoid *emotional buying* too. We get depressed and say, "I think I will go to the mall." At the end of the month, we will be even more depressed. There's a Greek word for this: Stupid!

Fourth, we must teach our people to give like a Christian. Tithing is a clear command in Scripture and a clear indicator of a Christian's spiritual health. Malachi 3:10-11 says, *Bring the whole tithe into the storehouse, that there may be food in my house. Test me in this," says the* LORD *Almighty, "and see if I will not throw open the floodgates of heaven and pour out so much blessing that there will not be room enough to store it. I will prevent pests from devouring your crops, and the vines in your fields will not drop their fruit before it is ripe," says the* LORD *Almighty.* Also, 2 Corinthians 9:6-7 states: *Remember this: Whoever sows sparingly will also reap sparingly, and whoever sows generously will also reap generously. Each of you should give what you have decided in your heart to give, not reluctantly or under compulsion, for God loves a cheerful giver.* Luke 6:30 offers another helpful teaching for Christians: *Give to everyone who asks you, and if anyone takes what belongs to you, do not demand it back.*

For some people, it takes almost a second conversion experience for them to trust God with their possessions. As A. W. Tozer once said, "There is no doubt that the possessive clinging to things is one of the most harmful habits in life. Because it is so natural, it is rarely recognized for the evil that it is – its out-workings are tragic. This ancient curse will not go out painlessly. The tough old miser within us will not lie down and die obedient to our command. He must be torn out – torn out of our hearts like a plant from the soil; he must be extracted in blood and agony like a tooth from the jaw. He must be expelled from our souls in violence as Christ expelled the money changers from the temple."[16]

We give our lives to the Lord. We trust Him to handle our spirit for all eternity. We give it all to the Lord, but when it comes to our money, we don't believe He can handle that! I don't ever dread preaching on giving. When I go to conferences, I tell the pastors that I love the subject. It blesses my people so much when they become obedient in their giving. In many churches, pastors are afraid to preach on giving because it may drive people away. During a series on this topic, we were blessed to have sixty-one new members come into the fellowship. Giving is at the heart of the gospel of Jesus Christ: *For God so loved the world that he gave his only begotten Son, that whosoever believeth in him should not perish, but have everlasting life* (John 3:16 KJV).

Tithing & Money

Several questions arise when considering how to be faithful with money as Christians, particularly regarding our giving.

First, how much should I give?

Sometimes people will make the mistake of saying they give

---

16 A. W. Tozer, *The Pursuit of God* (Harrisburg, PA: Christian Publications, 1948), Chapter 2.

the "widow's mite." I wish they did. Mark 12:41 says, *Jesus sat down opposite the place where the offerings were put and watched the crowd putting their money into the temple treasury.* I wonder what you would think if, when the offering is received on Sunday morning, I were to walk up and down the aisles and watch what you put in. You wouldn't want me tending to your business. But there is One who has the right to do that and does it – the Lord Jesus. The Bible says He was watching what they were giving.

More church members would stop tipping and start tithing if they remembered Jesus was watching. *Many rich people threw in large amounts. But a poor widow came and put in two very small copper coins, worth only a few cents. Calling his disciples to him, Jesus said, "Truly I tell you, this poor widow has put more into the treasury than all the others. They all gave out of their wealth; but she, out of her poverty, PUT IN EVERYTHING – all she had to live on"* (Mark 12:41-44, emphasis mine). I don't know many people who are willing to do what this woman did.

I've noticed that many times it's those who have the least who are the most generous in their giving. I know one couple who always gives the first tenth to the Lord. They came in one week and pledged five hundred dollars for our Academy, even though he was earning only five dollars an hour. That means he is giving a hundred hours above his tithe to the school for the glory of Jesus Christ. Some people have a dedication that goes far beyond what most people would ever understand.

Every Christian should give at least a tithe to the church. In my opinion, a biblical tithe is one-tenth of a person's income. Leviticus 5:11, Leviticus 6:20, Numbers 5:15, and Hebrews 7:2 all say that a tithe is a tenth. Some people object to the tithe because they reason that we are under grace, and tithing is a part of the Law of the Old Testament. Tithing is not Law; it was established before the Law was given to Moses. Genesis

14:20 says, *Abram* [that's before he was Abraham] *gave him a tenth of everything.*

Some people question whether tithing is taught in the New Testament. Tithing is reaffirmed in the New Testament, but even if it were not, I believe it would be a disgrace if we, under grace, would give less than the Jews gave under the Law. Jesus taught tithing in Matthew 23:23: *"Woe to you, teachers of the law and Pharisees, you hypocrites! You give a tenth of your spices – mint, dill and cumin. But you have neglected the more important matters of the law – justice, mercy and faithfulness. You should have practiced the latter, WITHOUT NEGLECTING THE FORMER* (emphasis mine). In other words, you should tithe, but don't think that by tithing you can pay God off. How you live is just as important as how you give.

Some Christians point out that this Scripture is the only place where the Lord endorsed tithing, along with the parallel passage in Luke 11:42. This suggests to them that the New Testament presents a weak case for tithing.

My question is, "How many times does Jesus have to say something before we believe it?" There is another passage mentioned by Jesus only one time. Jesus said in John 3:7, *You must be born again.* Obviously, this is an important truth! John 3:7 is central to the gospel of Jesus Christ. We preach and teach it. In regard to tithing, Jesus affirms it only once in God's Word. It is no less a weighty truth. Our Lord made no idle comments.

Interestingly, the same Greek word *dei* is used in both passages. It is translated "must" in regard to the new birth, but translated "ought" in regard to tithing. If translated literally, Matthew 23:23 would say, "You must not neglect the other." Just as important as the new birth is to salvation, so tithing is to living under the lordship of Jesus Christ.

To put it another way, tithing is not an adiaphoron – a thing indifferent. Examples of adiaphorons include: whether or not a minister wears a robe when he preaches; whether a person sits, stands, or kneels when praying; whether a church meets on a Friday or Wednesday for its weeknight Bible study or prayer meeting. These are things indifferent. Tithing is not like that – it's an absolute mandate!

Some people balk at the teaching on tithing because they believe they can't afford to tithe; they have too many bills. That's why we spend much time talking about how to earn your money, budget your money, and make your money count to the glory of the Lord Jesus. You don't need to be in financial bondage. You need to live in the free spirit of the Lord by living within your income. You don't live within your income unless you live on nine-tenths of what you are earning.

Others object to tithing because they do not know what the future holds. My question is, "Do you know Who holds the future?" In Malachi 3:8 we read about robbing God. But this passage goes on in verses 10-11 to say, *Test me in this," says the* LORD *Almighty, "and see if I will not throw open the floodgates of heaven and pour out so much blessing that there will not be room enough to store it. I will prevent pests from devouring your crops, and the vines of your fields will not drop their fruit before it is ripe," says the* LORD *Almighty.* We can trust God to provide for our future if we honor Him each day.

Years ago, I had the privilege of meeting Peyton Day, son of Cecil Day, the founder of Days Inn. Cecil died when he was forty-four years of age. He founded the Days Inn when he, with a large family, couldn't find an economical, clean hotel. He decided he would build one. When he was at Georgia Tech, Cecil and his wife struggled financially. But he insisted that the first tenth of everything they received went to the Lord Jesus. His wife argued with him saying they could not afford it. He countered that they could not afford not to.

After he died, they sold his chain of motels for $380 million.

Cecil Day not only tithed all of his income as he was receiving it, but he then left a mammoth estate for the Lord's work. After beginning at Georgia Tech and barely making ends meet, he made sure the first tenth went to the Lord, and the Lord blessed him beyond measure. You simply cannot out-give God.

I remember when I was a young preacher at New Smyrna Beach. A new Christian called me and said, "Pastor, I have enough money to either buy groceries for my family or give a check to the church for my tithe. Which should I do?"

He made sure the first tenth went to the Lord, and the Lord blessed him beyond measure.

Being of little faith, I said without hesitation, "You feed your family."

He thought a minute, and then said to me, "No, I feel impressed of the Lord to put Him first. I'm just going to trust Him to take care of things."

I was nervous about his decision. I didn't have that kind of faith myself. I was a preacher, but was young and immature. He wrote the check on Friday night to the church, and it exhausted their resources. He called me on Saturday and said, "Pastor, you won't believe what happened. Our next-door neighbors were moving to Kentucky, and they came over without even knowing we had a need. They offered us all the food in their freezer and cabinets so they wouldn't have to bother moving it."

Now, if the man had gone over and said, "We don't have any groceries, and my family is hungry," that would have been begging. The neighbor had no idea of the need, but God did. Not only did God supply their need, but He taught this preacher a lesson: not to question God's ability to take care of His children.

Second, when should I give my tithe?
First Corinthians 16:2 says, *On the first day of every week, each one of you should set aside a sum of money in keeping with your*

income, saving it up, so that when I come no collections will have to be made. There is a difference between a collection and an offering. A collection is an extraction – the church takes from the people. An offering is made when God's people are motivated by love to give unto the Lord. According to this verse, we are to give on the first day of each week – not at the end of the year as some people do. They use God's money all year, and then give to Him what is left over. When we write the first check every week to Jesus, it reminds us who is first in our life.

Third, what if I have not tithed for several years?

Malachi 3:8 says, *Will a mere mortal rob God? Yet you rob me. But you ask, 'How are we robbing you?' In tithes and offerings.* I believe, in all honesty, you should do what only one person I've known in my lifetime did. When he recognized what he owed the Lord, he gave land to catch up on the tithe. Catching up on past tithes will give us a clear conscience toward God, a conscience that is free of any guilt of robbing Him.

Fourth, should I tithe before or after taxes?

That's almost the first question asked by Christians who start tithing. I believe we should tithe on our income before taxes are taken because Jesus gets more that way. As God's people, we ought to do it the way He gets the most, not the way He gets the least.

Fifth, where should we give the tithe?

Malachi 3:10 says, *Bring the whole tithe into the storehouse.* There is a lot of argument in our day as to what is the storehouse. Many people send their money to television evangelists. I believe people should support their own local church with God's tithe. It is New Testament. The only "institution" established by Jesus was the His church.

In Matthew 16:18 Jesus said, *on this rock I will build my church.* He didn't say, "I'm going to build your church," or "You're going to build my church." He said, *I will build my church.* The church was established by God to carry on His mission in the world through the support of His people. There is accountability in the local church that you don't have with televangelists. Many of you saw the news report about the televangelist whose mail went directly to the bank. The prayer requests were tossed in the trash, and the checks were deposited. No accountability!

Now, if you have a love offering beyond the tithe, and God says to send it to Timbuktu, then you address the envelope to Timbuktu and send it. God will know where it goes. But when it comes to the tithe, the first tenth, it should to go to the local church. That is God's storehouse.

There are four surprises that will result as we are faithful in tithing:

(1) Once you begin tithing, you will be surprised at how trite the old excuses sound when you hear others use them. The excuses people give for not tithing have nothing to do with the Old Testament Law or New Testament doctrine. Those who don't tithe can't turn loose of the money because they don't love the Lord as much as they ought. It's just that simple.

When I first was saved, I loved money and had a real struggle with tithing. One Sunday my mother and father had given us our one-dollar allowance. My sister put the whole dollar in the offering plate. I thought she was insane! I went home and said, "Mom, do you know what Mary did? She took her whole dollar and put it in the church offering!" I had given a dime, but I really didn't do it joyfully. I wasn't a cheerful giver, so I can understand all the excuses.

(2) You will be surprised at the absolute joy that comes to your life when you are obedient to the Lord. Is there a gnawing restlessness in your soul? If you are not satisfied with your miserable life, it's because there is some area of disobedience. There is an area of resistance. But when you let go, you are

going to be surprised at the joy that comes from being totally obedient to the Lord.

(3) You will be surprised at how God meets your every need. My God shall not supply all of your greeds, but He shall supply all of your needs. When I graduated from seminary, the average income for people in my community was $30,000 a family. Our income was $3,600, and $1,200 of it went for a car payment and gas. We were left with $2,400, and we had three children. I did not know where the next dollar was coming from, but there was not a single time that we could not pay our bills, and we always had a shelter over our heads and clothes on our backs. Our God met every need according to His glorious riches.

(4) You will be surprised at how God will shower blessings on you beyond your needs. God has not only met my every need, but has blessed me personally through His people. God prompted my church family to do things that have absolutely confounded me and made me a believer in the providential care of God for His children. If you had told me twenty years ago that I would be as blessed as I have been, I would not have believed it. He has blessed me beyond measure, and I give Him the praise and glory for it.

One final text is Luke 6:38. This is a fantastic text. I want to share it in two different versions so we can get the complete meaning of it. Remember that the Living Bible is not a translation. It is a paraphrase, so don't ever use the Living Bible as a proof text. But at the same time, it gives a beautiful reading of this text. *For if you give, you will get! Your gift will return to you in full and overflowing measure, pressed down, shaken together to make room for more, and running over. Whatever measure you use to give – large or small – will be used to measure what is given back to you.*

Robert Gilmour LeTourneau, a business owner with earth-moving equipment, argued about that. He said, "That text is not true. God doesn't use the same measure in giving back." He said, "You know, I'd go out with my little old beach shovel, and I'd shovel to the Lord, and the Lord comes with His steam shovel, and He shovels it back to me." He says, "God hasn't used the same measure with me that I've used with Him."

In the New International Version, Luke 6:38 says, *Give, and it will be given to you. A good measure, pressed down, shaken together and running over, will be poured into your lap. For the measure you use, it will be measured to you.* Have you ever had so much fruit to carry that you would pull your shirt out in front to make a pouch? That's literally what this verse is talking about. Only this time we're talking about a robe, which will hold much more than a shirt. God is saying, "That's what I want to do for you." You'll be surprised at the blessing God will give you as you give to Him. I don't expect any of it. I don't give for that reason, and I'm always surprised when He does it. But He does it over and over and over again.

> *He didn't give a tenth or a portion. He gave His only Son.*

Conclusion

It all began with God giving to us two thousand years ago. *For God so loved the world, that he gave his only begotten Son.* He didn't give a tenth or a portion. He gave His only – one and only begotten Son *that whosoever believeth in him should not perish, but have everlasting life* (John 3:16 KJV). You see, you cannot even become a Christian without giving. You have to give yourself to Jesus, knowing He can do more with your life than you can. God loves you so much that He has given His one and only Son to die on the cross for you. Now He invites you to receive His Son and give your life to Him.

If you want to receive Christ as your Savior, the Bible tells us you must call upon the name of the Lord. God will honor your prayer, and as you reach up in faith, He is already reaching down in grace. At the moment the hand of grace and the hand of faith touch, the miracle of conversion will take place. God has given to us freely in Christ, and so too must we give with what God has given us. Money is something that God has given to us to use for *ministry evangelism* – to care for the poor and destitute. So of course we can afford *ministry evangelism* efforts if we are thinking, working, spending, giving, and leaving like a Christian.

I must conclude with a warning: It is good to have money and the things that money can buy, but it is good to check once in a while to see if by acquiring money and the fun things that money can buy, we have not lost the things that money cannot buy. I am reminded of the time that Thomas Aquinas was being escorted through the Papal Palace in Rome, and the Pope said, "No longer do we say, silver and gold have we none."

And Thomas said, "Neither can we say, rise, take up your bed, and walk." If you want to know your real worth, ask yourself what you have that money cannot buy, and death cannot take away. It's good to have money and the things that money can buy, but have we lost the things that money cannot buy?

Ministry Evangelism
in the Bible

———————— ∽ ————————

Exodus 3:7-8
The LORD said, "I have indeed seen the misery of my people in Egypt. I have heard them crying out because of their slave drivers, and I am concerned about their suffering. So I have come down to rescue them from the hand of the Egyptians and to bring them up out of that land into a good and spacious land, a land flowing with milk and honey—the home of the Canaanites, Hittites, Amorites, Perizzites, Hivites and Jebusites.

Leviticus 19:9-10
When you reap the harvest of your land, do not reap to the very edges of your field or gather the gleanings of your harvest. Do not go over your vineyard a second time or pick up the grapes that have fallen. Leave them for the poor and the foreigner. I am the LORD your God.

Numbers 20:15-16
Our ancestors went down into Egypt, and we lived there many years. The Egyptians mistreated us and our ancestors, but when we cried out to the LORD, he heard our cry and sent an angel and brought us out of Egypt.

Deuteronomy 10:17-19
For the LORD your God is God of gods and Lord of lords, the

great God, mighty and awesome, who shows no partiality and accepts no bribes. He defends the cause of the fatherless and the widow, and loves the foreigner residing among you, giving them food and clothing. And you are to love those who are foreigners, for you yourselves were foreigners in Egypt.

Joshua 20:9
Any of the Israelites or any foreigner residing among them who killed someone accidentally could flee to these designated cities and not be killed by the avenger of blood prior to standing trial before the assembly.

Judges 6:9
I rescued you from the hand of the Egyptians. And I delivered you from the hand of all your oppressors; I drove them out before you and gave you their land.

Ruth 2:2
And Ruth the Moabite said to Naomi, "Let me go to the fields and pick up the leftover grain behind anyone in whose eyes I find favor."

1 Samuel 2:7-8
The LORD sends poverty and wealth; he humbles and he exalts. He raises the poor from the dust and lifts the needy from the ash heap; he seats them with princes and has them inherit a throne of honor. "For the foundations of the earth are the LORD's; on them he has set the world.

2 Samuel 12:1-7
The LORD sent Nathan to David. When he came to him, he said, "There were two men in a certain town, one rich and the other poor. The rich man had a very large number of sheep and cattle, but the poor man had nothing except one little ewe lamb he had bought. He raised it, and it grew up with him and his children. It

shared his food, drank from his cup and even slept in his arms. It was like a daughter to him.

"Now a traveler came to the rich man, but the rich man refrained from taking one of his own sheep or cattle to prepare a meal for the traveler who had come to him. Instead, he took the ewe lamb that belonged to the poor man and prepared it for the one who had come to him."

David burned with anger against the man and said to Nathan, "As surely as the LORD lives, the man who did must die! He must pay for that lamb four times over, because he did such a thing and had no pity."

Then Nathan said to David, "You are the man! This is what the LORD, the God of Israel, says: 'I anointed you king over Israel, and I delivered you from the hand of Saul.

1 Kings 17:15-16

She went away and did as Elijah had told her. So there was food every day for Elijah and for the woman and her family. For the jar of flour was not used up and the jug of oil did not run dry, in keeping with the word of the LORD spoken by Elijah.

2 Kings 4:1-7

The wife of a man from the company of the prophets cried out to Elisha, "Your servant my husband is dead, and you know that he revered the LORD. But now his creditor is coming to take my two boys as his slaves."

Elisha replied to her, "How can I help you? Tell me, what do you have in your house?"

"Your servant has nothing there at all," she said, "except a small jar of olive oil."

Elisha said, "Go around and ask all your neighbors for empty jars. Don't ask for just a few. Then go inside and shut the door behind you and your sons. Pour oil into all the jars, and as each is filled, put it to one side."

She left him and afterward shut the door behind her and her sons. They brought the jars to her and she kept pouring. When all the jars were full, she said to her son, "Bring me another one." But he replied, "There is not a jar left." Then the oil stopped flowing. She went and told the man of God, and he said, "Go, sell the oil and pay your debts. You and your sons can live on what is left."

1 Chronicles 16:19-22
When they were but few in number,
few indeed, and strangers in it,
they wandered from nation to nation,
from one kingdom to another.
He allowed no man to oppress them;
for their sake he rebuked kings:
"Do not touch my anointed ones;
do my prophets no harm."

2 Chronicles 28:14-15
So the soldiers gave up the prisoners and plunder in the presence of the officials and all the assembly. The men designated by name took the prisoners, and from the plunder they clothed all who were naked. They provided them with clothes and sandals, food and drink, and healing balm. All those who were weak they put on donkeys. So they took them back to their fellow Israelites at Jericho, the City of Palms, and returned to Samaria.

Ezra 9:7-9
From the days of our ancestors until now, our guilt has been great. Because of our sins, we and our kings and our priests have been subjected to the sword and captivity, to pillage and humiliation at the hand of foreign kings, as it is today.
"But now, for a brief moment, the LORD our God has been gracious in leaving us a remnant and giving us a firm place in his sanctuary, and so our God gives light to our eyes and a little relief in our bondage. Though we are slaves, our God has not forsaken us in our bondage. He has shown us kindness in the sight of the

*kings of Persia: He has granted us new life to rebuild the house
of our God and repair its ruins, and he has given us a wall of
protection in Judah and Jerusalem.*

Nehemiah 10:31b
*Every seventh year we will forgo working the land and will can-
cel all debts.*

Esther 9:22c
*He wrote them to observe the days as days of feasting and joy
and giving presents of food to one another and gifts to the poor.*

Job 24:1-6
*"Why does the Almighty not set times for judgment?
Why must those who know him look in vain for such days?
There are those who move boundary stones;
they pasture flocks they have stolen.
They drive away the orphan's donkey
and take the widow's ox in pledge.
They thrust the needy from the path
and force all the poor of the land into hiding.
Like wild donkeys in the desert,
the poor go about their labor of foraging food;
the wasteland provides food for their children.
They gather fodder in the fields
and glean in the vineyards of the wicked.*

Psalm 9:18
*But God will never forget the needy;
the hope of the afflicted will never perish.*

Psalm 140:12
*I know that the LORD secures justice for the poor
and upholds the cause of the needy.*

Proverbs 14:31
*Whoever oppresses the poor shows contempt for their Maker,
but whoever is kind to the needy honors God.*

Ecclesiastes 4:1

*Again I looked and saw all the oppression that was taking place
under the sun:
I saw the tears of the oppressed –
and they have no comforter;
power was on the side of their oppressors –
and they have no comforter.*

Isaiah 1:15-17

*When you spread out your hands in prayer,
I hide my eyes from you;
even when you offer many prayers,
I will not listen.
Your hands are full of blood!
Wash and make yourselves clean.
Take your evil deeds out of my sight;
stop doing wrong.
Learn to do right; seek justice.
Defend the oppressed.
Take up the cause of the fatherless;
plead the case of the widow.*

Isaiah 11:4a

*but with righteousness he will judge the needy,
with justice he will give decisions for the poor of the earth.*

Isaiah 58:6-7

*"Is not this the kind of fasting I have chosen:
to loose the chains of injustice
and untie the cords of the yoke,
to set the oppressed free
and break every yoke?
Is it not to share your food with the hungry
and to provide the poor wanderer with shelter –
when you see the naked, to clothe them,
and not to turn away from your own flesh and blood?*

Jeremiah 22:2-3

Hear the word of the LORD to you, king of Judah, you who sit on David's throne – you, your officials and your people who come through these gates. This is what the LORD says: Do what is just and right. Rescue from the hand of the oppressor the one who has been robbed. Do no wrong or violence to the foreigner, the fatherless or the widow, and do not shed innocent blood in this place.

Lamentations 3:34-36

To crush underfoot
all prisoners in the land,
to deny people their rights
before the Most High,
to deprive them of justice –
would not the Lord see such things?

Ezekiel 16:48-50

As surely as I live, declares the Sovereign LORD, your sister Sodom and her daughters never did what you and your daughters have done.
Now this was the sin of your sister Sodom: She and her daughters were arrogant, overfed and unconcerned; they did not help the poor and needy. They were haughty and did detestable things before me. Therefore I did away with them as you have seen.

Daniel 4:27

Therefore, Your Majesty, be pleased to accept my advice: Renounce your sins by doing what is right, and your wickedness by being kind to the oppressed. It may be that then your prosperity will continue.

Joel 2:18-19

Then the LORD was jealous for his land
and take pity on his people.

The LORD replied to them:
"I am sending you grain, new wine and oil,
enough to satisfy you fully;
never again will I make you
an object of scorn to the nations.

Amos 2:6-7a
This is what the LORD says:
"For three sins of Israel,
even for four, I will not relent.
They sell the righteous for silver,
and the needy for a pair of sandals.
They trample on the heads of the poor
as upon the dust of the ground
and deny justice to the oppressed.

Obadiah 1:10-14
Because of the violence against your brother Jacob,
you will be covered with shame;
you will be destroyed forever.
On the day you stood aloof
while strangers carried off his wealth
and foreigners entered his gates
and cast lots for Jerusalem,
you were like one of them.
You should not look down on your brother
in the day of his misfortune,
nor rejoice over the people of Judah
in the day of their destruction,
nor boast so much
in the day of their trouble.
You should not march through the gates of my people
in the day of their disaster,
nor look down on them in their calamity

in the day of their disaster,
nor seize their wealth
in the day of their disaster.
You should not wait at the crossroads
to cut down their fugitives,
nor hand over their survivors
in the day of their trouble.

Micah 2:7-10

You descendants of Jacob, should it be said,
"Does the LORD become impatient?
Does he do such things?"
"Do not my words do good
to the one whose ways are upright?
Lately my people have risen up
like an enemy.
You strip off the rich robe
from those who pass by without a care,
like men returning from battle.
You drive the women of my people
from their pleasant homes.
You take away my blessing
from their children forever.
Get up, go away!
For this is not your resting place,
because it is defiled,
it is ruined, beyond all remedy.

Habakkuk 2:9

Woe to him who builds his house by unjust gain,
setting his nest on high
to escape the clutches of ruin!

Zechariah 7:8-10

And the word of the LORD came again to Zechariah: "This is what the LORD Almighty says: 'Administer true justice; show mercy and compassion to one another. Do not oppress the widow or the fatherless, the foreigner or the poor. Do not plot evil against each other.'

Malachi 3:5

"So I will come to put you on trial. I will be quick to testify against sorcerers, adulterers and perjurers, against those who defraud laborers of their wages, who oppress the widows and the father-less, and deprive the foreigners among you of justice, but do not fear me," says the LORD Almighty.

Mark 10:17-24

As Jesus started on his way, a man ran up to him and fell on his knees before him. "Good teacher," he asked, "what must I do to inherit eternal life?"

"Why do you call me good?" Jesus answered. "No one is good – except God alone. [19] You know the commandments: 'You shall not murder, you shall not commit adultery, you shall not steal, you shall not give false testimony, you shall not defraud, honor your father and mother.'"

"Teacher," he declared, "all these I have kept since I was a boy."

Jesus looked at him and loved him. "One thing you lack," he said. "Go, sell everything you have and give to the poor, and you will have treasure in heaven. Then come, follow me."

At this the man's face fell. He went away sad, because he had great wealth.

Jesus looked around and said to his disciples, "How hard it is for the rich to enter the kingdom of God!"

The disciples were amazed at his words. But Jesus said again, "Children, how hard it is to enter the kingdom of God!

Luke 10:29-37

But he wanted to justify himself, so he asked Jesus, "And who is my neighbor?"

In reply Jesus said: "A man was going down from Jerusalem to Jericho, when he was attacked by robbers. They stripped him of his clothes, beat him and went away, leaving him half dead. A priest happened to be going down the same road, and when he saw the man, he passed by on the other side. So too, a Levite, when he came to the place and saw him, passed by on the other side. But a Samaritan, as he traveled, came where the man was; and when he saw him, he took pity on him. He went to him and bandaged his wounds, pouring on oil and wine. Then he put the man on his own donkey, brought him to an inn and took care of him. The next day he took out two denarii and gave them to the innkeeper. 'Look after him,' he said, 'and when I return, I will reimburse you for any extra expense you may have.'

"Which of these three do you think was a neighbor to the man who fell into the hands of robbers?"

The expert in the law replied, "The one who had mercy on him."

Jesus told him, "Go and do likewise."

John 6:9-13

"Here is a boy with five small barley loaves and two small fish, but how far will they go among so many?"

Jesus said, "Have the people sit down." There was plenty of grass in that place, and they sat down (about five thousand men were there). Jesus then took the loaves, gave thanks, and distributed to those who were seated as much as they wanted. He did the same with the fish.

When they had all had enough to eat, he said to his disciples, "Gather the pieces that are left over. Let nothing be wasted." So they gathered them and filled twelve baskets with the pieces of the five barley loaves left over by those who had eaten.

Acts 2:44

All the believers were together and had everything in common.

Romans 12:13

Share with the Lord's people who are in need. Practice hospitality.

1 Corinthians 16:1

Now about the collection for the Lord's people: Do what I told the Galatian churches to do.

2 Corinthians 9:7-15

Each of you should give what you have decided in your heart to give, not reluctantly or under compulsion, for God loves a cheerful giver. And God is able to bless you abundantly, so that in all things at all times, having all that you need, you will abound in every good work. As it is written:
"They have freely scattered their gifts to the poor;
their righteousness endures forever."
Now he who supplies seed to the sower and bread for food will also supply and increase your store of seed and will enlarge the harvest of your righteousness. You will enriched in every way so that you can be generous on every occasion, and through us your generosity will result in thanksgiving to God.
This service that you perform is not only supplying the needs of the Lord's people but is also overflowing in many expressions of thanks to God. Because of the service by which you have proved yourselves, others will praise God for the obedience that accompanies your confession of the gospel of Christ, and for your generosity in sharing with them and with everyone else. And in their prayers for you their hearts will go out to you, because of the surpassing grace God has given you. Thanks be to God for his indescribable gift!

Galatians 2:10

All they asked was that we should continue to remember the poor, the very thing I had been eager to do all along.

Ephesians 4:28

Anyone who has been stealing must steal no longer, but must work, doing something useful with their own hands, that he may have something to share with those in need.

Philippians 1:9-11
And this is my prayer: that your love may abound more and more in knowledge and depth of insight, so that you may be able to discern what is best and may be pure and blameless for the day of Christ, filled with the fruit of righteousness that comes through Jesus Christ – to the glory and praise of God.

Colossians 4:1
Masters, provide your slaves with what is right and fair, because you know that you also have a Master in heaven.

1 Thessalonians 3:12
May the Lord make your love increase and overflow for each other and for everyone else, just as ours does for you.

1 Timothy 5:8
And anyone who does not provide for their relatives, and especially for their own household, has denied the faith and is worse than an unbeliever.

Titus 1:8
Rather, he must be hospitable, one who loves what is good, who is self-controlled, upright, holy and disciplined.

Philemon 1:15-19
Perhaps the reason he was separated from you for a little while was that you might have him back forever – no longer as a slave, but better than a slave, as a dear brother. He is very dear to me but even dearer to you, both as a fellow man and as a brother in the Lord.

So if you consider me a partner, welcome him as you would welcome me. If he has done you any wrong or owes you anything, charge it to me. I, Paul, am writing this with my own hand. I will pay it back – not to mention that you owe me your very self.

Hebrews 10:34
You suffered along with those in prison and joyfully accepted

the confiscation of your property, because you knew that you yourselves had better and lasting possessions.

James 2:14-17

What good is it, my brothers and sisters, if someone claims to have faith but has no deeds? Can such faith save them? Suppose a brother or a sister is without clothes and daily food. If one of you says to them, "Go in peace; keep warm and well fed," but does nothing about their physical needs, what good is it? In the same way, faith by itself, if it is not accompanied by action, is dead.

1 John 3:16-17

This is how we know what love is: Jesus Christ laid down his life for us. And we ought to lay down our lives for our brothers and sisters. If anyone has material possessions and sees a brother or sister in need but has no pity on them, how can the love of God be in that person?

1 John 4:19-20

We love because he first loved us. Whoever claims to love God yet hates a brother or a sister is a liar. For whoever does not love their brother or sister, whom they have seen, cannot love God, whom they have not seen.

Revelation 14:13b

"Yes," says the Spirit, "they will rest from their labor, for their deeds will follow them."

APPENDIX 2

Ideas for
Ministry Evangelism[17]

————————⸺∽⸺————————

The possibilities for ministry are endless. The following list is meant to help you get started. Some ideas are more applicable than others to your church and community.

Ministries to Parents and Married Couples

- Parents' Day Out: Provide child care one or more days a week, funded by a small charge to parents and by scholarships.
- New Parents: Provide babysitting for new parents.
- Family Seminars: Offer help with family issues such as discipline, safety, and nutrition.
- Couples' Supper Club: Organize groups of couples to meet in homes to share meals and enjoy Christian fellowship.
- Marriage Enrichment Seminars, Studies, and Retreats: Arrange opportunities for married couples to develop strong marriages; advertise in the community.
- Parenting Seminars, Studies, and Retreats: Provide information to enrich parenting skills; advertise in the community.
- Cradle Roll: Visit homes of new parents, enroll the baby, and give a pink or blue Bible.

17 Atkinson and Roesel, *Meeting Needs Sharing Christ*, 159-168.

- Premarital Counseling and Seminars: Provide guidance for couples considering or preparing for marriage.

Ministries to Women

- Pregnancy Care: Offer free pregnancy tests, counseling, and prenatal care. Include nutritional and parenting assistance.
- Shepherding Expectant Mothers: Furnish temporary care in the homes of church families for homeless, pregnant women.
- New Mothers: Prepare and deliver packets containing such items as a bib, a pink or blue Bible, a coupon for a home-cooked meal to be delivered when needed, *ParentLife* magazine, and information about the church.
- Single Mothers: Support and nurture with encouragement, fellowship, seminars, and emergency child care.
- Clothing: Supply appropriate work clothing for indigent women seeking employment.

Ministries to Men

- Single Fathers: Support and strengthen with encouragement, fellowship, seminars, and emergency child care.
- Clothing: Supply appropriate work clothing for indigent men seeking employment.

Ministries to Children

- Day Care: Provide a regular program of care, funded by tuition costs.
- School Clothing: Collect, purchase, and distribute school clothing for underprivileged children.
- Hospital Activity Packs: Prepare and deliver packs to hospitalized children and include such items as Bibles,

coloring books, crayons, small stuffed animals, puzzle books, and Christian books. Be sure to check with hospital personnel.

- Children's Care: Provide temporary shelter, food, and protection for children in crisis.
- Latchkey Ministry: Offer before- and after-school care for a small fee.
- Summer Day Camp: Present an opportunity for disadvantaged children to learn and grow. Include recreation, Bible study, and evangelism.
- Vacation Bible School: Using a planned curriculum, make Bible study and activities available to children.
- Backyard Bible Clubs: Organize neighborhood Bible clubs for children.

Ministries to Youth and Students

- Tutoring: Provide a free after-school program to help students with academic problems.
- Youth Prayer Breakfast: Prepare a free breakfast for youth once a week, including Christian fellowship and witness.
- Students Away: Encourage students with literature, personal letters, and encouragement through volunteers.
- Campus Reading Room: Make a reading room available near a school with volunteers to interact with students and answer questions.
- Seekers: Invite students to a forum where they ask questions about Christianity and interact with Christian students.

Christian School

- Teen Drivers: Offer a car-care-and-safety course including a Christian testimony.

- Teen Club: Provide Friday- and Saturday-night social events with food, fun, and a Christian witness. This activity must be carefully planned and supervised.

Ministries to Senior Adults

- Adult Day Care: Provide for those who need care while adult children fulfill other responsibilities.
- Home Meal Delivery: Cook and deliver hot meals.
- The Homebound: Arrange visitation, spiritual help, and practical ministry to those unable to attend church services.
- Nursing Homes: Plan worship, Bible study, prayer, visitation, and encouragement for residents of nursing homes.
- Grandparenting Seminars: Offer seminars on grandparenting and advertise in the community.
- Transportation: Provide transportation for grocery shopping, medical appointments, and church attendance.
- Activities: Plan regular programs of meaningful study and activity.
- Retirement Centers: Provide worship services for retirement centers which include music and testimonies.
- Shopping and Errand Service: Run errands and shop for the homebound.
- Lawn Care: Provide lawn care permanently or temporarily as needed.

Ministries to Single Adults

- Home Care: Provide home repair, especially for widows, elderly people, and single mothers.
- Car Repair: Offer automobile repair, especially for widows, elderly people, and single mothers.

Ministries to Special Needs

- Deaf People: Create a Sunday school class and discipleship training group and provide interpretation of worship services.
- Blind People: Supply tapes of worship services and other events.
- Caregivers: Provide temporary relief for caregivers of people with special needs.

Health Care Ministries

- Christian Health Program: Offer weekly sessions at the church.
- Aerobics: Organize aerobics classes at the church. The trained leader should be sensitive to participants' needs and should provide time for prayer requests.
- People with AIDS: Provide help and encouragement for patients and their families.
- Health Screening: Conduct screenings for blood pressure and cholesterol in disadvantaged neighborhoods.
- Bloodmobile: Have the Red Cross bloodmobile come to the church. Advertise hours to the community. Provide refreshments and Christian tracts for blood donors.
- Flu Shots: Provide free flu shots at the church for the community, working with the local health department.

Sports Ministries

- Athletic Events: Sponsor an event such as a walk/run or a softball tournament for the purpose of witnessing.
- Young Athletes: Organize clinics for young baseball, soccer, football, and tennis players. Invite a Christian athlete to give a testimony.

- Golfers: Sponsor a golf tournament and invite people who need Christ to participate. Share a Christian testimony.
- Athletes: Hold a pizza party for local high school or college teams with an opportunity for sharing Christ.
- Athletic Teams: Offer exercise, competition fellowship, and a Christian witness through team sports.
- After-Game Celebrations: Provide food and fun for a high school team in a Christian atmosphere.

Ministries to the Community

- Food Baskets: Prepare and distribute baskets of food to needy families during holidays and at other times.
- Christmas Toy Store: Purchase and collect new toys and other children's items and arrange the merchandise like a store. Invite parents who cannot afford to buy Christmas gifts for their children to come and select items free. Plan a Christian witness to the parents before they leave.
- Financial Seminars: Offer help with debt, budgeting, and planning.
- Home Bible Study: Invite neighbors to a home Bible study on a weeknight or a weekday morning.
- Income Tax Assistance: Provide free help with income tax preparation at the church during specific advertised hours.
- Bereavement: Prepare meals and other services for families or individuals in bereavement.
- Sympathy Notes: Mail a sympathy note to the family of every person whose name appears in the obituary column of the newspaper. This activity could be done by a group such as a Sunday school class or by an individual.
- Financial Assistance: Distribute funds to people with

basic financial needs such as rent, utilities, food, and prescriptions.

- Food Pantry: Distribute food from donations and government commodities.
- Clothes Closet: Distribute clean, wearable, used clothing.
- Families of Prisoners: Provide encouragement, spiritual help, and physical resources for families who have loved ones in prison.
- Personal Care Kits for Prisoners: Include toothpaste, toothbrush, soap, shaving cream, candy, gum, and Christian literature. Be sure to check with institutional authorities before assembling the kits.
- Prayer Breakfasts: Invite community residents to pray for community needs once a week at the church or at a local residence. Bible study could be included.
- Buses: Use church-owned or privately owned vehicles to provide transportation to church activities.
- Prayer: Mobilize the church to pray for needs in the church and community.
- Truck Stops: Provide Christian literature and fellowship for long-distance truck drivers.
- Counseling: Offer group or individual counseling by a professional counselor or by trained lay counselors.
- Decision Counseling: Counsel people making a decision for Christ.
- Holiday Meals: Provide meals for the homeless on holidays or at other times.
- Resorts: Offer Bible study or worship services at a nearby resort.
- Prisoners: Provide visits, Bible study, worship, and literature to people in prison.

- Special Events: Witness and minister at special community events. For example, maintain a booth at a community festival and serve free beverages. Be sure to obtain permission first.

- Literacy: Teach people to read and in the process share Christ with them.

- Christmas Gift Wrapping: Supply free or inexpensive gift wrapping in a mall. Distribute tracts and witness.

- Christian Fellowship: Plan a block party with food, entertainment, and a Christian witness for people in the neighborhood.

- Crafts and Cooking Classes: Offer classes for the community. The leader should be sensitive to participants' needs and provide a time for prayer requests.

- New Residents: Distribute kits for new residents. Include a city map; lists of hospitals, dentists, and physicians; shopping and school information; a gift certificate for a meal at a local restaurant or a coupon for a home-cooked meal; information about the church; and a Christian magazine. Invite new residents to be guests at the church's Wednesday night dinner.

- Fellowship Lunch: Invite working people to a fellowship lunch once a week that includes Bible study and prayer.

- Public Service Personnel: Host an appreciation day for law enforcement personnel and firefighters.

- Bibles: Give Bibles to groups such as college students, military personnel, firefighters, members of athletic teams, law enforcement officers, or nurses.

- Twenty-Four-Hour Prayer Line: Organize and advertise a telephone line that is staffed twenty-four hours a day. Receive prayer requests and pray.

- Hospitality: Serve meals in a family setting for students, military personnel, and business people away from home.
- Sewing and Knitting: Make lap robes, booties, and other articles to give away.
- Snow Removal: Recruit volunteers for a snow-removal brigade that services walks and driveways at the homes of the elderly, single mothers, the disabled, and non-Christians. Leave a note stating that this act was done in Jesus' love.
- Christian Tapes: Develop a library that includes audiotapes on biblical subjects, life issues, and music. Make the tapes available to church members to share with unchurched family members and friends.
- Disaster Relief: Develop teams and resources to work with denominational and community agencies to assist victims of disasters.
- Car Wash: Provide a free car wash, accepting no payment other than thanks. Serve lemonade to customers. Share that Christ's love is the reason for offering this service.
- Church Computer Bulletin Board: Reach out electronically.
- Birthday Cards: Send birthday greetings with Christian messages to as many unchurched people as possible.

Ministries to Internationals

- Language Skills: Teach people to read and speak English. Bible study and worship in the native language could also be provided.
- Women's Cultural Fellowship: Plan a weekly or monthly fellowship time for women from different countries to learn about American culture and one another's culture. Provide assistance with tasks such as grocery shopping.
- Home Hospitality: Deliver meals to homes of families or individuals who have recently arrived from other countries.

Ministries Through Church Programs

- Musical Productions: Use seasonal musical productions such as a living Christmas tree to provide a Christian witness.

- Saturday Sunday school: Organize and present a Saturday Bible study program for children from disadvantaged circumstances.

- Sidewalk Sunday school: Use a portable classroom to take Bible study to neighborhoods in the inner city or in unchurched areas.

- Music: Use choirs, ensembles, and other groups to involve children, youth, adults, and senior adults. Have groups perform in public places, providing the opportunity to share a Christian witness.

- Drama: Use drama to involve interested people and to present the gospel.

- Puppetry: Use puppets to involve those who wish to present the gospel in this manner, especially to children.

Support-Group Ministries

- Divorce Recovery: Offer help for people who are divorced or who face divorce.

- Sexual Abuse: Support, aid, and arrange help for people who are victims of sexual abuse.

- Grief Recovery: Provide comfort and assistance for people who have experienced losses in their lives.

- Chemical Addiction: Arrange support for people who are recovering from addiction to alcohol or other drugs.

- Codependency: Establish help for people who are dealing with issues of codependency.

- Eating Disorders: Support, encourage, and locate help for people recovering from eating disorders.

About the Author

D r. Roesel's rich past includes being the recipient of the Southern Baptist Distinguished Service Award. In addition to all other ministries, Dr. Roesel had a television ministry reaching out to four million homes each week. In 1973, he was chosen as Florida's Urban Pastor of the Year by Stetson University.

First Baptist Church of Leesburg, Florida thrived under Dr. Roesel's thirty-year leadership, and is now considered the model for *ministry evangelism*. In a town of 15,000 with over ninety churches, the church grew by transformation, baptizing over 7,000 people.

First Baptist Church of Leesburg, Florida now has over seventy separate ministries including The Men's Residence, Women's Care Center, Children's Shelter Home, Benevolence Center, Furniture Barn, Food Pantry, Teen Shelter, Pregnancy Care Center, Medical Center, Counseling Center, Preschool, First Academy Leesburg (K-12th Grade), School of Fine Arts, Rape Crisis Center, Aides Clinic, Mentoring Program, Children-at-Risk Program, Mentally Challenged, People Helpers (Counseling), Signing Ministry, a Home Ministry sharing with over four hundred home-bound persons each week, and more.

Connect with Dr. Roesel
www.ministryevangelism.org

For more personal testimonies about the effectiveness of *ministry evangelism*, visit: www.ministryevangelism.org

Never before have we seen the church degenerate at such a rapid pace. This is largely due to the church pursuing congregational growth instead of kingdom growth. The church is dying because our growth isn't based on strategies to reach the lost with the gospel. The time to change is now, we can't wait any longer. People's eternities are at stake.

What is your church's priority? Are you more concerned with filling your building or furthering the Kingdom? This book will challenge you to evaluate just how important gospel-based evangelism is to you and your church, and call on you to restore an intentional evangelism strategy within the body. Hell will tremble when churches once again make evangelism the central theme of their strategy.

Available wherever books are sold

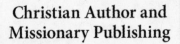